MINDING
MY OWN
Healing

MINDING MY OWN

Healing

A **PERSONAL JOURNEY** AND
COMPANION FOR NAVIGATING THE
HEALING PROCESS AFTER
PAST TRAUMA, PAIN, OR
BROKENNESS

MELANIE SMILES

MINDFUL MISSIONS

MINDING MY OWN HEALING

The information provided in this book is simply the personal experience and journey of the author, with emotional, physical, and spiritual healing. This book is not meant to be used, nor should it be used to diagnose, treat, cure, or prevent any disease or medical condition. This information has NOT been evaluated by the FDA. The content in this book is not intended as a substitute for the medical advice of a physician. The reader should regularly consult with their doctor in matters relating to his/her health and particularly with respect to any symptoms that may require diagnosis, medical attention, or mental health services.

Paperback ISBN: 979-8-218-46660-2
First Paperback Edition: August 2024
Printed in the United States of America

Edited by: Khloe's Thoughts Editing
Cover by: Make Your Mark Publishing Solutions
Layout by: Make Your Mark Publishing Solutions

Contents

Acknowledgements

All praises and thanks to my Heavenly Father. I am so grateful for the countless blessings you have bestowed upon me, including my family, friends, and my faith. I am humbled by your presence in my life, and I do not take anything for granted. I am thankful for the opportunity to learn, grow, and heal from the things I have experienced. I pray I may always strive to honor and serve you to the best of my ability. I pray to be a positive influence and light in this world and to bring hope and healing to those around me.

Special thanks to my mother Pearlene, sister Chef Kim, and entire family for your overwhelming support in everything I do. Thank you to everyone that poured into me, encouraged, prayed, and interceded on my behalf. Dr. Laticia Beatty, Maurice Edley, Teresa Creggett, Tamika Henry, Alajia Turner; thank you for being a part of this journey to help bring hope, encouragement, inspiration, and healing to this world. Thank you to all the nurses, doctors, healthcare professional, mental health care techs, police officers, firefighters, EMS, DFD, and health care workers across the globe; you make a difference in this world. Detroit DMC Sinai Grace nurses, DEMS, and DPD— you guys rock!

Introduction

As I was minding my own healing, I learned that healing is personal. It's the body's physical or emotional response to injury. In life, I learned sometimes bad things must happen before good things can. Healing is a spiritual and emotional journey. Healing is a personal process of becoming whole or healthy again that involves physical, mental, emotional, and spiritual experiences.

We never perceive brokenness or something bad as good until later when we see the good thing that came from the bad thing. Sometimes the bad situations that happen in our lives put us on the right path to the best thing that will happen to us and position us for healing in certain areas of our lives.

In relation to this book and my journey, healing is the process in which a bad situation or emotional trauma ends or improves. Healing doesn't mean forgetting or ignoring the pain, it's when the pain no longer controls you. You can detach from what has been inflicted and only take the lesson with you.

As you journey through these pages and lessons I learned while I was minding my own healing, I want you to know healing is not a destination but an ongoing path of growth, self-care, and refinement. It's a process that takes time filled with many days that are up and down, but you must keep going.

My prayer is that the words, information, scriptures, and

testimonies of the contributing authors poured into this book encourage and motivate you to navigate through your healing journey of past trauma, pain, or brokenness. When the spirit of heaviness and life's issues arrive, I hope this book is a source of inspiration and companion to live life in purpose, on purpose.

Some say time heals all wounds, that's not true. Time alone does not heal you; you heal you. It is important to have the right heart posture to be successful in your healing journey. Abundant fruit comes when we assume the right heart posture. Posture of the heart refers to its position and condition. God has already given us His healing power and placed it on the inside of every believer. It's up to us to access it and release it.

The pain and hurt may not have been my fault, but healing is my responsibility. My proverb is "Hurt people hurt others, but healed people heal others."

> For I will restore health to you and heal your wounds, says the Lord," (Jeremiah 30:17).

> He heals the brokenhearted and binds up their wounds," (Psalm 147:3).

> Behold, I give you the authority to trample on serpents and scorpions, and overcome all power of the enemy, and nothing shall by any means hurt you," (Luke 10:19).

MELANIE SMILES

Melanie Smiles is a bestselling author, a registered nurse, specializing in emergency and trauma nursing, and the owner of Mindful Missions Health & Wellness. As a God-fearing and caring woman who has triumphed through the struggles of teenage motherhood and narcissistic abuse, Melanie has the gift to serve. She has an unwavering desire to be a woman of influence by helping others overcome brokenness so they can heal and live a more peaceful, fulfilled life by sharing the good works of Jesus Christ.

Chapter One

SPIRITUAL FOUNDATION

hen I began minding my own healing, I learned building a strong spiritual foundation was necessary and I needed to recognize and acknowledge that I was broken and needed healing. Your spiritual life is the most important because it controls every other area of your life. I understand spirituality is a broad concept that may mean different things to different people. In general spirituality is a personal and inward journey characterized by our faith and belief that includes a sense of connection to something bigger than ourselves. Our spiritual life helps shape our lives, values, beliefs, desires, how we live, how we deal with the issues of life, and the choices we make. The word "foundation" is defined as the ground or the lowest part of a structure before it is made, and all the other parts are laid upon it. In the natural world if the foundation of a building is not properly laid the structure can collapse, and the same in the spiritual world. A weak, cracked, or wrong foundation will result in disaster or brokenness. A strong spiritual foundation helps you navigate and support you from all seasons and forces of life that will come.

> *Why do you call me, 'Lord, Lord,' and do not do what I say? As for everyone who comes to me and hears my words and puts them into practice, I will show you what they are like. They are like a man building a house, who dug down deep and laid the foundation on rock. When a flood came, the torrent struck that house but could not shake it, because it was well built. But the one who hears my words and does not put them into practice is like a man who built a house on the ground without a foundation. The moment the torrent struck that house, it collapsed, and its destruction was complete,"* (Luke 6: 46-49).

Before God saved me, I was spiritually broken. My spiritual foundation was weak and had many cracks in it. My brokenness was a doorway for the adversary to seep through the cracks and present himself as an angel of light, having access to my mind and emotions, breaking and exposing other broken areas of my life. We know that brokenness interrupts our lives and separates us from anything that keeps us from living our best lives, leaving a person feeling discouraged, unhappy, hopeless, incomplete, depressed, or wounded. Satan uses our brokenness as a window of opportunity to enter our lives, causing negative thoughts that can lead to bad actions or more pain. I know from experience that whatever gets your mind gets you. The battle for sin always starts in the mind. When the spirit is weak, the mind run errands for the flesh by thinking negative thoughts.

> For as he thinks in his heart, so is he." (Proverbs 23:7).

Therefore, as believers, it is important to make sure that our spirits are strong. The Apostle Paul said that we are transformed by the renewing of the mind (Romans 12:2).

> Be alert and of sober mind. Your enemy the devil prowls around like a roaring lion looking for someone to devour. Resist him, standing firm in the faith, because you know that the family of believers throughout the world is undergoing the same kind of sufferings," (1 Peter 5:8-9).

The devil is real, and he won't show up in a red suit with a pitchfork and horns. He is right here on earth with us and shows up in many forms, looking for someone to devour. In the book of Job, God asked *Satan, "From where do you come? So Satan answered the LORD and said, "From going to and fro on the earth, and from walking back and forth on it,"* (Job 1:7).

Satan knows he cannot devour just anyone; therefore, he looks for ways to access us and gain a foothold in our life through brokenness, sin, relationships, trauma, negative thoughts, unhealthy desires, addictions, insecurities, fears, ignorance, environments, and other areas. We know that once the devil has a welcome invite and has a foot in our door, he will wreak havoc in our life and will not leave nicely. He is your adversary; his goal is to keep you broken and ultimately destroy you. The good news is while I was minding my own healing, I learned the devil is a liar, a deceiver, and already a defeated foe. Jesus not only took away our sins at the cross, but He also redeemed you from Satan's power and dominion.

> *He who sins is of the devil, for the devil has sinned from the beginning. For this purpose the Son of God was manifested, that He might destroy the works of the devil."* (1 John 3:8).

Early on in my journey to healing, I had to first acknowledge I was broken and remove myself from what was breaking me. You really can't rebuild yourself in an environment that ultimately destroyed or is destroying you. We cannot heal in the same environment that broke us or traumatized us because those environments are triggers and can be unsafe. Healing also cannot come from the source of injury or the person that hurt you. They may express remorse, apologize, change their actions, but they lack the capacity to heal you. You heal you. Emotional and spiritual healing is an inside job. On your journey to healing you must begin with creating a safe place.

During my healing journey and strengthening my spiritual foundation, God placed some amazing and influential people in my life. My mother and family were there to comfort, support, and pray for me. My aunt, Evangelist Juanita Cross, who was also my spiritual mother, who is now in heaven, consistently planted the word of God in me. Close friends adopted my burdens in prayer, provided an ear while I vented out my frustrations, and gave me wise counsel. My church was a safe haven for worship, prayer, and spiritual growth.

I was inspired greatly by our first Lady of PCBC Jodi Matthews, who is also one of our Sunday school and Bible teachers where I learned, grew, and went deeper into the fundamentals of Christian education. Lady Jodi is the author of *Revelation, Simply Put,* it is the first visual commentary on the Book of Revelation. She is an amazing woman of God, servant leader, influencer, and is passionate about teaching the word of God. She inspires youth, is a frequent life-changing speaker for churches, faith-based institutions, United Conference For Women, and various media platforms.

Minister Laticia Beatty, who is now known as Dr. Laticia Beatty was one of my greatest influencers along my spiritual walk— healing, encouraging, and helping cultivate my gifts. Dr. Beatty is a registered nurse, minister, philanthropist, entrepreneur, author, mentor, faith coach, and founder of Speaklife Network and Ministries. Although me and Dr. Beatty went to the same high school, we really didn't know each other, she was a couple grades higher than me. I became connected with her through a travel business opportunity, which led me to what I believe me being her assignment.

As I was minding my own healing, I learned our life is not our own. We all have purpose and assignments in life. When a person is assigned to you, they selflessly add value to you. They pour, sow, and make deposits into someone spiritually, emotionally, and sometimes physically. They serve in love, invest their time, pour wisdom, knowledge, love, resources, and what they have received from something or someone. They are simply anointed to enrich other people's lives. People that are anointed to you or anointed for an assignment comes from God and not of man. Since they come from God, they are blessed and come with the power to perform their assignment.

> He who calls you is faithful, who also will do it," (1 Thessalonians 5:24).

> The generous soul will be made rich, and he who waters will also be watered himself," (Proverbs 11:25).

I was not only Dr. Laticia Beatty's assignment, but she also gave me practical assignments for my spiritual growth. She emphasized the importance of having a strong spiritual foundation because it is the key and essential for healing, building relationships, business, ministry, and it starts within us.

As you begin or continue your healing journey, identify a Dr. Laticia Beatty, Jodi Matthews, or a person of profound influence that leads by example to help you navigate through your spiritual healing, cultivate your gifts, and help you become the best version of yourself. When life seems confusing and the road gets tough, which it will, having someone there to encourage you from a spiritual perspective can help you stay in alignment with God, your purpose, your passion, and your healing.

As I was minding my own healing, I learned you can't follow just any influencer or allow anyone to pour into you. Everyone that mentors, coaches, influencers, or has a big social media following isn't anointed to and may have other motives. Some will see gifts and talents in you that you don't see and use them for their benefit. They will prostitute your gift so that it works for them and not you. Therefore, you should check their fruit, pray, and ask God to send you someone, give you eyes to see, ears to hear, and see what He sees, and align you with someone that can meet you right where you are, edify you, draw you closer to Him and not of man, and that their motives come from the Holy Spirit and not of their flesh.

Chapter Two
REJECTION

Minding my own healing, I learned rejection is inevitable. It's a natural part of life everyone will experience at some point, and it can be very painful. Rejection is an emotional wound. Psychologist, Guy Winch, shared that when scientists placed people in functional MRI machines and asked them to recall a recent rejection, they discovered something. The same area of our brain becomes activated when we experience rejection as when we experience physical pain. That's why sometimes even small rejections hurt more than we think they should because they elicit literal (emotional) pain. It makes you feel like you are not good enough or not important. If not dealt with properly, the spirit of rejection will start prophesying lies to you. Instead of you are fearfully and wonderfully made with a future and hope, you are worthless, nobody wants you, and your future is not looking so bright. The fruit of rejection looks different on everybody. It comes in the form of shame, jealousy, anxiety, addiction, depression, anger, embarrassment, people pleasing, or makes you feel like someone else is better than you, even when you give your best.

There have been countless times in my life I have experienced rejection from relationships to workplace discrimination and social settings. As a teenage mother of two kids, I experienced rejection from friends and their parents not wanting them to hang around me because they felt I was a bad influence on their child. Early motherhood for sure had its challenges, but I was determined to become someone many people thought and said I would never be.

All rejection and disappointment hurt. In my experience, relationship rejection was the most painful. The pain from feeling rejected in my marriage broke me all the way down to my knees. When my marriage spiraled downward and I found out about all the bad and hurtful things my now ex-husband did to me, at one point, the devil tried to infiltrate my mind to make me think something must be wrong with me to make my husband cheat, lie, disrespect, and emotionally abuse me. Those thoughts were so far from the truth, the devil is a whole lie and the truth is not in him. The devil is so deceitful; he will create a lie in your head that's in your own voice. Do not let the devil plant that seed in your head you're not good enough. Some rejections truly aren't as personal as they feel. That person could have been thinking he/she will not be good enough for you. You may intimidate them or they may not be ready for who you might become. You may have thought, "I've done all these good things for them, I'm a whole wife/husband, no drama, beautiful, successful, great cook, loving with a good heart and they just threw me away," or "My best wasn't good enough; I'm a good person, I did everything they asked and more and it still wasn't good enough for them to love me properly." Why not? I learned God may not want them to see you were a good person and will allow us to experience rejection to protect us. He will withhold your gifts and hide your value from people because He knows they would have used and manipulated you for their benefit.

I learned I don't need closure, answers, or need to get an understanding from the one that rejected or hurt me. When I was frustrated, the pain only deepened when I tried to make sense out of something that didn't make sense. Even if they ghosted you, it is ok, Let them go! Do not chase after them, don't go back and try to make it right, demand answers, or try to get revenge. When people ghost you and don't care about you, they don't care if you are angry at them. If they don't care about you, you can't hurt them even if you try, so don't. Save your energy and your peace because it will only deepen your pain, especially if they don't respond to your revenge the way you wanted them to. Let it go, and trust God is protecting you from something you can't see because your emotional feelings for them may have blinded you from seeing the red flags.

> Consider it pure joy, my brothers and sisters, whenever you face trials of many kinds, because you know that the testing of your faith produces perseverance. Let perseverance finish its work so that you may be mature and complete, not lacking anything," (James 1:2-4).

> *When my father and my mother forsake me, Then the Lord will take care of me,"* (Psalm 27:10).

Rejection is the opposite of being accepted, but rejected doesn't define your value as a person. Somehow, we feel since we have been rejected, we're not important or less valuable, and that's not true. It just means at that particular time, situation, season, person, or thing didn't work out, or you were excluded from. It doesn't mean I'm not blessed, favored, loved, beautiful, or smart. You can be the ripest, sweetest, and juiciest peach in the world, and there's still going to be people who don't like peaches, no matter what. They may like strawberries and apples instead. Their choice is not a reflection of you. Rejection is hardly ever about you, but more about them.

Rather than focusing on what might be wrong with you (there's nothing wrong with you but this is where we tend to go) focus on what you can learn from the person or experience. Are there any red flags that you missed? (more than likely there were).

By reflecting in this way, you're looking to improve your experiences rather than put it on yourself as a failure.

I couldn't see it then when I was going through my dark season. Now I look back and see there were red flags I overlooked. But God knew all along what I needed to go through to bring me to my knees and draw me closer to Him. As painful as it was, my brokenness and rejection were a blessing from God because it redirected me to Him. In the process of my rejection, I have learned that God rejects those things that limit, block our blessings, hold us back, and stand in the way between us and Him.

I was reminded by a saying an old friend once told me, "If you lose yourself to gain the love or attention from someone else, you lose. But if you lose that person but found you, or that relationship draws you closer to God then you are the winner." I am the winner!

Chapter Three

PRUNING IS PAINFUL

> I am the true vine, and my Father is the gardener. He cuts off every branch in me that bears no fruit, while every branch that does bear fruit he prunes so that it will be even more fruitful. You are already clean because of the word I have spoken to you. Remain in me, as I also remain in you. No branch can bear fruit by itself; it must remain in the vine. Neither can you bear fruit unless you remain in me," (John 15:1-4).

Minding my own healing, I learned when it comes to pruning or cutting away dead things, rather it's relationships, friendships, old mind-sets, or old ways of operating, this process is necessary. There will come a time when God needs to let go, cut certain people and things out of our lives to sustain our growth and healing. It's then when God will allow us to experience a season of pruning because He is preparing us for something greater. He knows there are some people, things, and attitudes we need to let go of before we enter our next season. We are going to go through many pruning seasons in our life, and because it can be so painful it may feel like God is punishing us through the process, but it's actually the complete opposite because He loves us. He loves us so much that He doesn't want us carrying around those dead branches weighing us down that keep us from bearing fruit. He wants us to grow, be productive, heal properly, and bear plentiful fruit.

Once a seed is planted and germinated, its roots are established into the ground, and it starts to grow upward. The vine as Jesus calls himself, produces branches— which are believers like you and me get life from the vine. These branches are then pruned, which is the process where a gardener "Our Father" removes parts of a plant or tree like buds or dead leaves. These parts are usually removed because they cause more harm than good to the overall plant. A plant will continue to send water, energy, and nutrients to its dead parts, depriving the living and growing parts of what it needs. A gardener must frequently go out and cut off any dead leaves or fruitless branches because they are taking nutrients that should be growing and producing more fruit.

Dealing with the brokenness and the aftermath of a failed marriage, I was reminded I had to let it go. I had to let go of the anger, disappointment, shame, and things my ex-husband and others did that hurt me. Trying to hold on to all those negative things wasn't going to make things better or move me toward the new things God had for me. Had I continued to hold on and stay in that broken and toxic place, it would've continued to die and probably taken me along with it. I was in a toxic and unsafe space. It began to infect every area of my life including my health, work, family, and business. It wasn't God honoring. I spent years walking on eggshells, never doing or saying the right thing. It was clear I needed to let it all go. One day I decided I'd had enough and stomped all over them. Those broken eggshells cut me deeply as I walked away, but that was the most beautiful pain I had ever felt.

> Come to me, all you who are weary and burdened, and I will give you rest. Take my yoke upon you and learn from me, for I am gentle and humble in heart, and you will find rest for your souls. For my yoke is easy and my burden is light," (Matthew 11:28-30).

God literally allowed my life to be flipped upside down; I was so broken I didn't think a shattered piece of glass like me was fixable. Through my brokenness and pruning, I could see I was being shaped and molded into what He has called me to be. Through the process is when you can see this amazing transformation that has happened in our life as God prunes us.

As we grow, heal, and mature in Christ there are many things that stifles our continued growth and spiritual maturity. There were other things I had to let go of— like going out to nightclubs, especially ballroom dance nights, hanging with certain people, going to certain places, stop watching, listening, and entertaining certain things because it wasn't fruitful for what God wanted to do with me.

Afflictions and pruning are never comfortable and can come in many forms of loss or suffering. That's the part of spiritual growth we don't like. Sometimes it may come in the form of a test after test. Remember, God tests but the devil tempts us.

> When tempted, no one should say, "God is tempting me." For God cannot be tempted by evil, nor does he tempt anyone, (James 1:13).

Temptation itself is not sin or bad: it is something we all encounter simply by being human. It is submitting to the temptation that causes the sin. A person's inner nature and desires determine what he/she is tempted by on the outside. Temptation is being enticed or influenced to sin or things that are not favorable to us. Temptation intensifies when God is refining us. Tests are designed for you to pass by responding with the right choice. God will provide what you need to pass the test. In the natural realm we go to school, learn the lesson, and then take the test. But with God in the spiritual realm, we get tested first then learn the lesson. I learned the hard way. If you're not learning the lesson God is trying to teach you, He'll allow you to retake the test. If you don't pass it the first time, you'll get another chance and another chance and another until you do pass. God doesn't do this to punish us, He's trying to reveal our weakness and sin, so that we seek Him to learn how to overcome it and pass the test. We don't pass spiritual tests in our own strength, rather on God and obedience to Him because through Him nothing is impossible. God never asks us to carry our burdens and fight our battles in our own strength. He asks us to give our burdens to Him. Psalm 55:22 tells us, *"Cast your cares on the Lord and he will sustain you; he will never let the righteous be shaken."*

> Consider it pure joy, my brothers and sisters, whenever you face trials of many kinds, because you know that the testing of your faith produces perseverance. Let perseverance finish its work so that you may be mature and complete, not lacking anything," (James 1:2-4).

> Blessed is the one who perseveres under trial because, having stood the test, that person will receive the crown of life that the Lord has promised to those who love him," (James 1:12).

One of the ways to distinguish a test vs temptation is the source and the outcome. How do you pass the test or pruning phase? Seek Him, pray, be obedient to His word, you hold on, you keep going, you press on, keep the faith, and stand on God's promises. You can seek therapy and wise counsel if needed. Put down that baggage of the past and step into a better future. Let go of what God needs you to release and trust God will continue what He started in you.

> *Being confident of this, that he who began a good work in you will carry it on to completion until the day of Christ Jesus,"* (Philippian 1:6).

Chapter Four

YOU DON'T HAVE TO BE PERFECT TO BE POWERFUL

> So God created mankind in his own image, in the image of God he created them; male and female he created them," (Genesis 1:27).

> For we are God's handiwork, created in Christ Jesus to do good works, which God prepared in advance for us to do," (Ephesians 2:10).

We've all had a taste of insecurity, doubt, uncertainty, and perfectionism which somehow all seem to stem from a lack of confidence within ourselves, shame, or fear. To be insecure is to lack confidence, not having confidence in who you are and why God created you. Our insecurities are birthed through what we allow ourselves to believe. One of Satan's biggest weapons is doubt. Satan loves for us to question who we are and how we measure up to others.

Minding my own healing, I learned sometimes when individuals experience insecurity, they seek validation and self-worth in their achievements that possibly can lead to perfectionism. As an unwed, teenage mother of two kids in high school it brought on its challenges of insecurity, feelings of shame, embarrassment, and disappointment. I was frowned upon, stigmatized, judged harshly, and people looked at my pregnancies as a mistake. I didn't get to experience prom, homecoming, or other events. I didn't get to enjoy my pregnancy like some older women do, no one celebrated it with me bedside at my baby shower. Instead, people talked down about me, repeatedly reminding me how I threw my life away. Some of my friends' parents shamed me and didn't want their child no longer hanging around me because they felt I was a bad influence on them. As if keeping their child from being my friend or hanging around me would stop them from getting pregnant, but I got the message. I knew I disappointed my parents and let them down. I refused to lay in the hole I dug myself. Being a mom is not easy at any age, but being a teen mom is very rough and scary because you're still learning and growing and need a strong support system. I was determined to be successful, prove everyone wrong who spoke failure over me, cast me out, and nailed me to the cross.

At some point, I came to realize God doesn't make mistakes. I did, and that pregnancy was a gift from God, even when it didn't look like it from where I was standing. I decided I was going to change the negative narrative people spoke over my life into something positive. With the support of my family, I was able to graduate high school on time, complete cosmetology school and became a licensed cosmetologist, run a hair salon business, went back to college, received several certificates and a degree in nursing while working full time at a country club. I felt achieving success was a way for me to cover up the shame and right my wrong of being a teen mom. Finally, I had found a sense of normalcy and belonging after being criticized, condemned, and judged for so long. However, doing that brought on the spirit of perfectionism, not spending enough time with my kids, and fear of failing again. My fear was that if I don't do it perfectly or good enough it will expose my inner weakness and shame me all over again.

Perfectionism is often seen as a positive because these individuals are usually high achievers and very successful. However, there can be a dark side to perfectionism that keeps you in bondage. Perfectionism can work as bondage by always pushing us to do better and more. When we are constantly trying to achieve more and better, we are not free. Being a perfectionist is extremely challenging and draining, both to yourself and the people around you. In extreme form, it can lead to depression, anxiety, eating disorders, and other mental health problems.

Psychology Today states perfectionism is a response to inner shame that often comes from childhood trauma. Experts state perfectionism is the belief that everything must be perfect all the time. I became focused on what others thought of me, what the world considers is right, where I need to be and doing with my life. The constant fear of failure, not getting things right, people pleasing, needing to be in control of everything and striving to do everything right left me exhausted mentally, physically, and emotionally.

> *Whatever you do, work at it with all your heart, as working for the Lord, not for human masters, since you know that you will receive an inheritance from the Lord as a reward. It is the Lord Christ you are serving,"* (Colossians 3:23-24).

Minding my own healing, I learned to pursue the spirit of excellence and not perfectionism. Perfectionism operates from the need to do everything right; Excellence is about doing the right thing. A spirit of excellence is anchored to the things of God, it's the key that will help bring you through trials and tribulations. Excellence is an attitude and heart posture. With excellence, you may strive to do your best, but you also allow yourself grace, remain in peace, accept failure, and mistakes as you learn from them. I thought by doing things perfectly I would be in control, could ensure my own security with others, and get things done on my own. A spirit of excellence is knowing I cannot do it on my own and rely on God's help, favor, grace, and strength. I had to stop trying to fix every little thing I thought was wrong in my life and sometimes other people's lives.

I am learning that when you lay your burdens at the feet of Jesus and leave it there, when you cast your cares unto the Lord and allow Him to take the spotlight in your life, you are breaking free from the weight and the chains of perfection. We serve a perfect God, but He does not require perfectionism from us. As you are minding your own healing journey, remember God has never called us to be perfect. If you're going for perfection, it's a destination you will never reach. Instead, we should strive for excellence. Seeking excellence is a journey, not a destination.

We see these things displayed in the life of Daniel. The Bible says he had the spirit of excellence.

> Then this Daniel was preferred above the presidents and princes, because an excellent spirit was in him; and the king thought to set him over the whole realm," (Daniel 6:3).

Excellence says you've made mistakes, but you can learn from it. Excellence says God chose me, He called me, and He put his spirit within me. I am fearfully and wonderfully made; His works are wonderful. I don't have to be perfect to be powerful. You don't have to be perfect to be powerful.

Chapter Five

DISTRACTIONS

> Be alert and of sober mind. Your enemy the
> devil prowls around like a roaring lion look-
> ing for someone to devour," (1 Peter 5:8).

The Merriam-Webster's online dictionary defines distractions as something that turns your attention away from something you want to concentrate on. In other words, distractions are meant to shift our focus.

Minding my own healing, I learned some things about distractions; they have a purpose. Its purpose is to distract us from our purpose. The most dangerous kind of distraction shifts our attention from something of greater importance to something of lesser importance. When the enemy sends distractions, they never look like distractions until they are finished distracting you. They are not always obvious, clear, or evident. In fact, they often are rather unapparent and subtle. Distractions can come in the form of people, things, relationships, places, thoughts, circumstances, desires, environments, or temptations. They can come from different angles in ways we least expect from people we don't expect and at times we don't expect. They can end up costing us time, peace, relationships, money, success, and fulfillment.

We now live in a world where social media has dominated our lives. It shapes our behavior and influences our decisions. Most people are addicted to their smart gadgets, phones, and social media platforms only to look into other people's lives they're really not living. Social media robs us of precious time we can never get back. Social media can and has been a great way to stay connected with friends, family, and stay updated on news, information, and new ideas. However, social media can be a major source of distraction and waste of time. It can keep you from achieving your goal(s), being productive, and can be a hindrance to your healing— personal and professional growth.

Our attention often runs to what's important to us. Therefore, distraction can reveal what we love, desire, and our sinful nature. I remember one Sunday, our pastor was preaching a sermon. He stated something I will never forget. He said, "What we set our mind on in the beginning is not visible to anyone else. But when we feed it attention it will eventually become visible through our actions." That statement resonated with me for some time because what he said was true.

Minding my own healing, I embraced solitude. The constant exposure to endless stimuli of work, emails, smart phones, social media, notifications, entertainment, family, and relationship issues, were distractions and caused me to lose focus on goals, the inability to overcome challenges, get things done, and heal properly. Solitude granted me the gift of distance, allowed me to step back, remove myself from people, external distractions, and provided a space to recharge, gain perspective, focus, grow spiritually, find inner peace, and heal. Solitude heightened my self-awareness and allowed me to be in touch with my thoughts and emotions. Some people were offended by me doing this and took it personal as if it was directed toward them. It wasn't about them at all or what they thought. It was about me protecting my peace, creating a mind sanctuary, and cultivating a healthy and safe mental space. Apparently minding your business, staying to yourself, and not bothering people…bothers people. Unapologetically, do not let other people's personal feelings or thoughts about you stop you from creating that safe space, getting your cup filled, and cultivating the healing you need.

Minding my own healing, I learned you must be intentional about removing distractions. You can make plans on your day off to relax, meditate, read, or study your Bible, and as soon as you sit down, open your Bible— ready to receive a word— that's when your phone starts ringing, and text alerts come through. That phone hasn't rung all day, but as soon as you position yourself to hear a word from the Lord, here come the distractions. Being intentional, I had to turn the phone completely off and remove it from my presence until I was done. Hearing the message alerts and notifications made me feel pressured to respond to messages or emails. Having it on vibrate was also a distraction because I could still hear it. Having it on silent didn't work either because the phone would still light up. I could see notifications come through and I would pick up the phone. Next thing you know, I'm replying to texts, calls, and emails, which one time led me to engaging in conversation with someone lasting almost an hour. While I was on that call, another call came in from my hairstylist stating she can fit me in to get my hair done if I could come within the next hour. I ended up getting dressed without any further thought of reading the Bible and headed to the hair salon. Defeated by the distractions, I didn't get a chance to open my Bible and study as planned for several days later.

I state be intentional about eliminating distractions because the enemy knows that if we're constantly distracted by the noise of the world, it will keep us from hearing the voice of God. In other words, keep the main thing, the main thing. It's important to identify your distractions because everyone is not distracted by the same things. For example, having my phone close by, the television on, or playing music when reading or studying is a distraction for me. While others actually concentrate better when there is background noise. You do not want to be that person so caught up with distractions, working, and worldly influences, then only acknowledge God right before bed, before eating, or when in a desperate situation and need of a prayer request.

FASTING

Minding my own healing when fasting— solitude, identifying my distractions, and removing external distractions are one of the things I look forward to. Fasting is a spiritual discipline that involves eliminating distractions and desires for a spiritual purpose; it hits the reset button of our soul and renews us from the inside out. As your body becomes free from the inside, your mind does as well. Fasting helped me trust God on a deeper level. It humbled me, helped me focus, and revealed what was controlling me. Fasting also revealed what and who I gave power to. Fasting is not just about sustaining from certain food, drink, or temptation, rather it's the impact and breakthroughs that can be gained through the experience.

Before you fast start with a clear goal, be specific. Why are you fasting? What are you believing God for as a purpose of your fast? Do you need direction, healing, restoration of marriage, relationship, or family issues? Are you facing financial difficulties? Ask the Holy Spirit for guidance – He will give it freely.

Chapter Six

SELF-CARE/SOUL-CARE

> *Do you not know that you are the temple of God and that the Spirit of God dwells in you?"*
(1 Corinthians 3:16).

> *Or do you not know that your body is the temple of the Holy Spirit who is in you, whom you have from God, and you are not your own? For you were bought at a price; therefore, glorify God in your body and in your spirit, which are God's,"* (1 Corinthians 6:19-20).

Minding my own healing, I learned self-care isn't selfish, it's necessary and there is healing power in it. It involves listening to your body and taking care of your physical, mental, and emotional health. It helps you nurture and improve your overall health and well-being so that you're able to live and work in a more productive and fulfilling way. It also helps us show up as the best version of ourselves and enjoy better relationships with ourselves and others. Self-care can help heal external and internal wounds. Your body is a temple of God and belongs to Him. Therefore, take good care of it and use it for good purposes.

When I was going through my broken season, the effects of my *broken smiles* and life issues had me in such a dark place. I was married to a covert, narcissistic, sociopath that left me broken and traumatized. I was hurt, angry, and embarrassed. The effects of his emotional abuse, toxic behavior patterns, and serial cheating infected every area of my life. In that same broken season, we lost the father who raised me since I was a toddler, my daughter's best friend was murdered, and my son was going through a crisis episode of bipolar depression. I had suffered from headaches and migraines for years, but they were becoming more frequent and lasting longer. I began having phases of dizziness with my headaches, which was unusual. I developed high blood pressure at stroke level with no history of hypertension. My hair started falling out in large patches, the more I combed the more came out. My nails were very brittle, my face was breaking out, I had no energy, I felt tired, I was drained, and depleted all the time. Everything that was happening on the inside of me was starting to reflect outwardly.

When our bodies repeatedly get weighed down by stress, emotional intoxication, or trauma, it will start to weigh in and wear you down. We all have an emotional or stress meter, and stress that goes unmanaged becomes distress. When the stress piles up and overloads us, a nervous breakdown or mental crisis may occur. I know from experience, sometimes we are met with unexpected or consecutive life events that we simply are not emotionally prepared to manage and unable to process properly. I learned you must be careful not to allow life stress to pile up and weigh in on you.

It's ok to be sad at times, it's ok to not be ok because we're human beings and it's a part of life. We're not designed to experience only positive emotions and feelings all the time. Having moments of sadness and grief doesn't mean you are not coping with a situation. The problem comes when we stay in that sad place too long. Through my healing process, I had to learn how to manage my sadness and emotions properly. I can't necessarily control what causes my stress, disappointments, and grief but I can control how I respond to it.

Minding my own healing, I learned most of the damage and pain that we endure from life's tests, trials and afflictions don't take you out, it's our response to it. When you can't control what's happening, challenge yourself to control the way you respond to what's happening, that is where your power lies.

When you are in a broken season it's easy to let yourself go and fall into the cracks of your broken spaces. As humans, we subconsciously look for ways to fill these cracks left by the breaks from others. Most of the time those cracks are filled with unhealthy things like sinful behaviors, jumping into a new relationship just to fill a void, codependency, binge eating, sexual affairs, drugs, and alcohol— which will only deepen your wounds and can significantly contribute to physical and mental illness.

Minding my own healing, I learned it was important for me to show kindness to myself and navigate the healing process in a healthy way. Even if it meant dating myself, dressing up just to go to the grocery store, not leaving out to run errands, wearing pajamas, a bonnet, not combing my hair, or missing out on events due to not having the energy to go anywhere. You can sometimes tell a lot about a person's outlook on life by how they take care of themselves. Some people look exactly like what they have been through or going through.

One of the first steps I took toward self-care was self-awareness and learning to embrace all my emotions and manage them properly. Even the ones that made me feel shame, weak, and painful. I became self-aware and practiced self-love. I started getting out of the house more, soaking up the natural sunlight, taking walks around the park and exercising while listening to music, sermons, and affirmations. I took myself out on lunch dates and tried out new restaurants and ate healthy foods. I dedicated a room to prayer, studying, and meditation. I challenged myself to devote time with God in that room every morning before the sun came up. The most impactful and liberating steps I took toward self-care and healing was reading my Bible and educating myself on narcissists and the effects of my brokenness. I had encountered a spiritual awakening moment. Educating myself on what was hurting me— narcissistic abuse— its behavior, and the traumatic effects it left on my life, allowed me to recognize the signs and traits associated with it. It helped me understand I was not alone and not to blame for his behavior toward me, but a reflection of what was going on with him and how he felt about himself. It helped me not only understand what was happening on a deeper spiritual and emotional level with narcissism but gave me knowledge and power to avoid it from happening again in the future.

MINDING MY OWN HEALING AND SETTING BOUNDARIES

I used to think setting boundaries and building a wall up were the same, they are not the same. Walls are not healthy; they can make you feel like a victim and are usually based on pain, fear, anger, used to make demands on people, control, and gives a false sense of safety. Walls disconnect, keep people out, and limit growth. Boundaries on the other hand are healthy personal rules or limits you establish to protect your well-being, maintain healthy relationships, and heal. Through boundaries you teach people how to treat you. I also used to think boundaries were selfish, and unconditional love meant unconditional tolerance, and that is so far from the truth. I love helping people. I have a giving and willing spirit and work hard to demonstrate commitment in many areas. It used to be hard for me to say "no" to people, especially to people I love, care about, and genuinely want to help out but can't. I don't like disappointing people or setting rules in relationships.

Minding my own healing, I learned fear of disappointing others can turn into people pleasing and that you can love someone to the moon and back and still have boundaries. Boundaries don't determine the amount of love you have in your heart. Setting boundaries is not selfish, you need boundaries to prioritize your peace and healing. You can love, empathize, be kind and be respectful, but set boundaries. In this way, you can love others while also taking care of yourself.

People would call or text asking when my next day off was so they could include me in their plans. For some reason, people tend to think your off day makes you available for them and their needs. As if you have nothing else going on in your life and waiting for others to pencil you into their schedule on your day off. I had to learn to say no I wasn't available even if I wasn't busy. That was a struggle for me because I used to equate not being available, to not being reliable or valuable, and that's not true. One of the tools I learned from a great speaker at a conference was that unless you are being paid to be on call 24/7, it's ok to not be available on your day off. It's ok to not answer your phone just to say, "I will call you back, I'm in the middle of doing something right now." Just wait until you are done and call them back when it's convenient for you. You are still valuable even when you are not available.

Minding my own healing, I learned brokenness and trauma

will allow others to drain you, deplete you, and make you tolerate a lot of things you don't deserve because you don't want to lose people. Boundaries and healing make you realize some people don't deserve access to you or be in your life no matter how much you love them.

Setting boundaries and guarding our hearts is about protecting ourselves from external and internal factors and influences. We must be mindful of who we give access to, allow to enter our hearts, and mind as well as people and things we give our attention and time to.

> Above all else, guard your heart, for everything you do flows from it," (Proverbs 4:23).

MINDING MY OWN HEALING THROUGH THE POWER OF MUSIC

Minding my own healing listening to music and audio Bible scriptures help to encourage and put me in a better mood. Music is powerful. It has the power to touch our souls, lift our spirits, and heal. Studies have also found listening to music helps release endorphins hormones associated with pleasure, which further reduces stress levels and may even aid in the healing process. It can improve your mental well-being, instantly create a feeling, a memory, a mood, or a passion. Music is often used in therapy sessions for several reasons; it helps create an atmosphere conducive to stress relief and healing emotional wounds.

Depending on what you are listening to, music can shift the feelings of a situation you are going through. It can change the heart's direction, focus, purpose, and create a change in someone's spirit, good or bad. In its purest form, I believe music is a precious gift from God, designed to uplift the thoughts, inspire, and elevate the heart. Music has long been used as a source of comfort and solace in times of distress. David played the harp and music for Saul's distressing spirit.

> But the Spirit of the Lord departed from Saul, and a distressing spirit from the Lord troubled him," (1 Samuel 16:4).

> And Saul's servants said to him, "Surely, a distressing spirit from God is troubling you. Let our master now command your servants, who are before you, to seek out a man who is a skillful player on the harp. And it shall be that he will play it with his hand when the distressing spirit from God is upon you, and you shall be well," (1 Samuel 16:15-16).

> And so it was, whenever the spirit from God was upon Saul, that David would take a harp and play it with his hand. Then Saul would become refreshed and well, and the distressing spirit would depart from him," (1 Samuel 16:23).

Negro spirituals are songs created by the Africans who were

captured and brought to the United States to be sold into slavery. While on the plantation, spiritual songs sustained Africans when they were enslaved. The songs were a way of lamenting, expressing their faith, hope, prayer, and worship. They would sing these songs in church and in the work field. In the church, it evolved into gospel songs. In the fields, it became what we know now as the blues. Some of the lyrics use Biblical imagery expressing the desire for a release from bondage.

Spiritual songs were also used to communicate with one another without the knowledge of their masters. For example, it was said Harriet Tubman used the song, *Wade in the Water,* to tell escaping slaves to get off the trail and into water to make sure the dogs' slave catchers couldn't sniff out their trail. *Go Down Moses* was a song that Harriet Tubman used to signal to other slaves that she was in the area. Some historians also believed in reference to the song, *Go Down Moses,* that Harriet Tubman was interpreted as the Moses of their days. Harriet Tubman was one of the leaders of the Underground Railroad, along with a group of abolitionists, both Black and white, formed a network of transportation and safe houses that assisted slaves in their escape from southern plantations. *Hush, Somebody's Calling My Name* alerted other slaves that one of them was getting ready to run, so pay attention. *Swing Low, Sweet Chariot* had references to desiring freedom or death from slavery.

The spiritual songs they created while in slavery helped give them hope and life in the midst of bondage and abuse. They saw the power of music and how it made them feel. Negro spirituals strengthened and firmed slaves' faith, who may not have been able to see imminent freedom, hoped and believed that freedom was possible.

Music is a powerful spiritual tool, which can be used by both the evil kingdom and the heavenly kingdom. Most secular music played today has been tainted and are songs of debauchery that glorifies sex, money, drugs, degrading women, hate, power, violence, and idolizing ourselves. Some lyrics glorify witchcraft, death, suicide, homosexuality, and even satanic entities. Secular music is the driving force behind a lot of crime, hate, jealousy, and demonic influences in the world. Satan also knows the power of music and uses it as an opportunity to keep people broken, promotes perversion and sin. Since music can infiltrate our minds, the adversary uses music as a vessel into the airways to gain access to people's minds and lives. Therefore, as believers, we cannot be ignorant of the effects music has on the heart, purposefully as you are navigating through a season of healing.

I learned you cannot entertain all music, especially in a season of brokenness. We tend to want to listen to music that can relate to what we are going through, good or bad. I remember a time in my season of brokenness, my *broken smiles* was causing me so much pain and the song, *Bust The Windows Out Your Car*, by Jazmine Sullivan came on one day. It encouraged me to go bust the frame and mirrors on one of his motorcycles. The lyrics in that song were so relatable, it was as though she felt every pain

I was feeling. I was so hurt by what he did to me, I wanted to teach him a lesson not to play with people's feelings and see what happens when you do. Motivated by the song, I walked out the side door, entered the garage, and grabbed one of his crowbars to demolish the motorcycle. As I was walking toward his motorcycle, he pulled up into the driveway. He got out of his truck and asked me, "Why are you outside this time of night with a crowbar in your hand?" I deflected his question by asking, "Where are you coming from at this time of night?" Thankfully, the Lord saved his little motorcycle that day from being demolished.

In my season of brokenness, I allowed a song to influence and motivate me to grab a crowbar with the intent on wrecking, dismantling, and annihilating someone else's property. This shows music has a way of doing something we can't see in the spirit realm; yet, it has consequences that show up in the natural world. Therefore, it is pertinent to your healing to listen to positive, uplifting, praise and worship music that is going to feed your spirit man, stimulate good things, activate the Holy Spirit, and get your spirit where it needs to be. Not music that pleases the flesh. Our ears are portals and what goes into our ears, goes into us, and can shift your mind and how you operate. We must guard our ear gates and be aware of the music and things we allow to saturate our hearts and minds.

As you are minding your own healing, take a moment to reflect on the lyrics in the music you listen to. Does it promote the fruit of the Spirit of God or the fruit of the flesh? Does it bring out good or evil? Does it encourage obedience to God, promote the desire to do right and bring forth positive change? When you listen to it, do you feel peace, anxiety, agitation, or anger? Does it put you in a better mood? Does your music build the love of God in your heart, or the love of the world?

MINDING MY OWN HEALING ON VACATIONS, TRAVELING, AND REST

Vacationing, traveling, and going to women empowerment conferences became my most essential and liberating form of self-care. Vacations are not just a way to escape from the stress or daily routine of life, but it is therapy for me. Being mindful, I asserted vacationing instead of taking a trip. Taking a trip is ok, my view of a trip can be any type of travel including business, family visits or weekend getaway, usually short duration and may not involve leisure, rest, or taking a break. On the other hand, to me a vacation is all about the experience. Traveling and vacation is my opportunity to take a break, disconnect and unplug from life's stressors to recharge. I love being by the ocean, waking up being kissed by the sunshine, being pampered and resting on vacation. I prioritize rest, it's not only a gift but also a weapon against the enemy. Overworking, always tired, and never taking a break keeps us in a weakened state and unable to be our best. If the enemy can keep you weary, tired, and unrested, he can remain undetected in areas of your life. Rest strengthens us, sharpens us and enables us to be more effective. Being well-balanced and rested is a threat to the enemy because he will not be able to gain access to your life easily.

Traveling as a form of self-care can have numerous benefits for maintaining health, both physically and mentally. Here are some of the key importance and benefits I found reading an article on WebMd website.

1. **Physical Activity**: Travel often involves exploring new places, which can require walking, hiking, swimming, or other physical activities. Engaging in these activities helps to keep the body active and promotes cardiovascular health.

2. **Stress Reduction**: Taking a break from the routine of daily life and experiencing new environments can reduce stress levels. Being in nature or visiting peaceful destinations can have a calming effect on the mind and body, lowering blood pressure and cortisol levels.

3. **Mental Stimulation**: Travel exposes individuals to new cultures, languages, and experiences, which can stimulate the brain and enhance cognitive function. Learning about different customs and ways of life can broaden perspectives and keep the mind sharp.

4. **Improved Mood**: Traveling often brings about feelings of excitement, anticipation, and happiness. The anticipation of a trip and the experiences gained during travel can boost your mood and overall well-being.

5. **Social Connections**: Traveling with friends, family, or even meeting new people while exploring can strengthen social bonds and create lasting memories. Positive social interactions have been linked to improved mental health and longevity.

6. **Sunlight and Vitamin D**: Many travel destinations offer ample opportunities for outdoor activities in the sun. Sunlight exposure is essential for the body to produce vitamin D, which plays a crucial role in bone health, immune function, and mood regulation.

7. **Break from Routine**: Breaking away from the monotony of daily life routines can provide a much-needed mental break. It allows individuals to recharge, gain perspective, and return to their regular lives with renewed energy and motivation.

8. **Cultural Immersion**: Experiencing new cultures can foster empathy, tolerance, and a deeper appreciation for diversity. Engaging with different traditions, cuisines, and

ways of life can broaden one's understanding of the world and promote personal growth.

9. **Mindfulness and Relaxation**: Traveling often encourages individuals to be more present in the moment, whether it's enjoying a beautiful sunset, savoring a delicious meal, or simply soaking in the surroundings. Practicing mindfulness during travel can promote relaxation and reduce anxiety.

10. **Inspiration and Creativity**: Exposure to new environments and experiences can spark creativity and inspire new ideas. Many artists, writers, and innovators find that traveling to different places enhances their creativity and provides fresh perspectives.

Overall, incorporating travel into one's life can contribute to overall health and well-being by promoting physical activity, reducing stress, stimulating the mind, fostering social connections, and providing opportunities for relaxation, personal growth, self-care, and healing.

I understand everyone is not able to take long vacations or have the financial means to take a vacation. Don't let your budget limit you in your pursuit of self-care and healing, where there is a will, there is a way. So often we say we can't afford to or we make excuses, but what it boils down to is that we haven't prioritized it. Yes, it can cost money, but it doesn't have to break the bank, and can be something you save up for. How bad do you want a vacation? You will be surprised how much money you spend on things like Amazon, Starbucks, DoorDash, Instacart, (their fees alone could probably get you a couple vacations) hair (them bundles prices is a whole flight), make-up, nails, eyelashes, entertainment subscriptions (including the ones you don't use) recreational drugs, and alcohol. A vacation doesn't have to cost a lot of money. You don't have to plan a fancy vacation; it all depends on what you want to get out of it. It can be a staycation. Taking a vacation or break from work is essential because it can reduce stress, help prevent burnout, and promote work-life balance by allowing time to recharge both physically and mentally and spend time with family and friends.

Stop putting off trips, travel, and vacations because it's not the right time or you're waiting for someone to go with you. Don't let other people decide what you do or don't get to experience in life. If you are always waiting for someone to travel with you, you may end up waiting a lifetime. It's not about having time, but about making time. Life is short so make the best of it, enjoy the time you have now and start living instead of just existing.

MINDING MY OWN HEALING
EATING FOOD FOR THE SOUL

Anyone that knows me knows I love to eat. Food is one of my love languages. I enjoy holidays, cookouts, family reunions, and Sunday dinners. Food is the ultimate expression of love and care. It is through the act of cooking and sharing meals we can show our affection for one another. There's nothing more fulfilling than to see my loved ones well fed, happy, and satisfied. Food has the magical ability to bring people closer together, whether it's a family dinner at home or a celebration with friends and coworkers. Sometimes, when food is offered, no words are needed. The down-home soul food cooking and traditions is a strong staple in our family with its identity deeply rooted in African American and southern culture. Commonly found on a soul food plate are fried chicken, ham hocks, smothered pork chops or chitterlings (chitlins), a green like kale or collards, fried okra, a bean like black-eyed peas or lima beans, mac and cheese, yams, and maybe some cornbread. Common desserts are pound cake, sweet potato pie, and peach cobbler. An ice-cold glass of red Kool-Aid or brewed iced tea are some traditional soul food beverages.

Although I was raised on eating soul food cooked and prepared by my parents and grandparents whose Mississippi southern roots, traditions, and love language was poured into every meal; I learned many healthy foods comprise soul food (collards, okra, rice, beans, and sweet potato). Soul food tends to be high in sugar, fat from various meats, especially pork, seasoned with lard or other animal fats. As a registered nurse, I'm aware that soul food and high consumption of southern diets are linked to an increased risk of several illnesses including hypertension, heart disease, strokes, obesity, vision problems, kidney disease, and is a huge problem in the African American community. An unhealthy diet can cause delay in healing, negatively impact your mental health, and cause worsening of symptoms of mood disorders such as depression.

Minding my own healing, I learned eating a healthy diet, detoxing, and getting adequate sleep can lead to better mental health. Eating a balanced and nutritious diet helps fuel our bodies and brains with the nutrients needed for proper function, which can improve our mood, energy levels, cognitive function, and physical and emotional healing.

Adopting eating healthy food and incorporating a few days of exercise into my weekly routine has unquestionably shown a positive effect in my healing journey.

In my early twenties, I developed a severe case of cystic acne. This wasn't the normal little acne pimples; these were big painful cysts with excessive oily skin that persisted no matter what acne medication or treatment I tried. I visited many dermatologists that prescribed treatments that consisted of injections in my face, chemical peels, topical gels, and a variety of oral medication only to be left with major scars, dark spots, and irritated skin. I also was having irregular menstrual cycles, painful cramping, and heavy bleeding. This went on for years, it was very depressing and embarrassing until I visited my gynecologist and shared my problems with her. She ran a few tests and informed me that I was battling a hormonal issue called polycystic ovarian syndrome (PCOS). She told me to modify my diet and gave me a prescription for oral contraceptives (birth control pill) and she wanted to reevaluate me in six months. God answered my prayers because that was the end of my battle with PCOS.

Polycystic ovary syndrome (PCOS) is a condition that causes hormonal imbalance and problems with metabolism. PCOS is a common health condition experienced in one out of ten women of childbearing age. Though the exact cause of this condition is still not clear, evidence have shown diet and eating habits has a significant role in PCOS and can lead to several other serious health challenges like diabetes, cystic acne, weight gain, fatigue, cardiovascular diseases, depression, infertility, and increased risk of endometrial cancer. Over recent years, PCOS has increased in adolescent girls that consume a poor diet, unhealthy food habits, and are obese. Those numbers are significantly higher in African American women.

Minding my own healing, I educated myself on PCOS. I learned most people with PCOS have elevated levels of chronic inflammation. There are two types of inflammation, acute and chronic. Acute inflammation is your body's natural response to illness, injury, or infection (germs) and usually resolves on its own. It promotes healing and helps you feel better. The other type of inflammation affects the whole body, it's called systemic. Systemic inflammation can become chronic and wreak havoc on your body, and even contribute to many other chronic diseases such as heart disease, arthritis, autoimmune disorders, asthma, diabetes, and others. Chronic low-grade inflammation in the body can be treated well with a proper diet.

Research shows diet, exercise, and regular checkups with a healthcare provider has been found to help women with PCOS manage their condition. I modified my eating habits and adopted healthier food choices, which have reduced inflammation and significantly improved my symptoms, if not eliminated them.

There is good evidence to support an anti-inflammatory diet or adding whole plant-based foods, such as those suggest Mediterranean plan or Dash diet help manage PCOS. These diets are balanced fiber-rich foods, healthy fats, and foods rich in anti-oxidants. All processed foods can cause inflammation. Therefore, focus on adding these foods into your daily diet.

- Whole grains such as oatmeal, brown rice, and quinoa.
- Non-starchy vegetables such as broccoli, green beans, and eggplant.
- Green leafy vegetables such as spinach, kale, and collard greens.
- Natural organic spices and herbs such as turmeric, ginger, cinnamon, and garlic.

- Legumes and pulses such as black beans, kidney beans, chickpeas, and lentils.
- Omega 3 fatty acids fish and shellfish.
- Nuts and seeds such as walnuts, pistachios, and sunflower seeds.
- Fruits, including a variety of berries, citrus fruits, and pomegranates.
- Organic cold press juices.
- Drink plenty of water.
- While you work on incorporating more nutritional foods, avoid or work on cutting back on these foods.
- Foods made with white flour including white bread, dinner rolls, pasta, crackers, and pizza crust.
- Sugary beverages like alcohol, soda, juices, iced tea, and energy drinks.
- Processed snacks including sugar, cookies, cakes, granola bars, and candy.
- Certain cereals include instant oatmeal with added sugar and granola.
- Fried foods (including French fries, fried chicken and fish, and potato chips).
- White rice.
- Excessive red meat including hamburger, pork, and steak.
- Processed luncheon meats, hot dogs, and sausage.

Being healthy doesn't mean you have to give up all the foods you enjoy eating (I still indulge from time to time), nor do you have to be perfect. It doesn't have to be hard, we're all busy. Start with adopting a positive and mindful approach to food. It's never too late to start undoing the damage caused by a poor diet. I learned getting healthy doesn't start in the gym, getting healthy starts in the mind.

Try new food options, explore different food cultures around the world, and learn the culture behind certain foods and how it's related to physical and mental health.

Food is an essential part of life, and without food, for me there wouldn't be an authentic healing experience. Limit your soul food intake but enrich your diet with food for your soul.

Being mindful, if you are under doctor's care and taking prescribed medication for high blood pressure, high cholesterol, diabetes, asthma, etc., understand medicine is not a substitute for unhealthy eating and lifestyle. A healthy diet and lifestyle changes are important even if you take medication. Studies show type 2 diabetes, hypertension, high cholesterol, respiratory diseases and others are commonly linked to poor diet, lifestyle, and physical inactivity.

Many people think overindulging in food like fried chicken, french fries, soda, cake, and ice cream is ok as long as they take their insulin, an extra pill, or other medicine. That's not true, your results won't be effective. It's like trying to put out a house fire with a squirt gun. A bad diet can cause harm no matter how much medicine you take.

Often patients come to the emergency room upset complaining about not feeling well, their blood pressure and blood sugar is high and stating their medication isn't working. After asking them a few questions, I learned many of them are not taking their medication as prescribed, they continue consuming a high sodium poor diet, illicit drugs and alcohol, smokes daily, and are not physically active. Many patients come in with difficulty breathing, COPD, or asthma flare with a known and frequent respiratory history that smokes daily, yet some will say their rescue inhaler or medication isn't working or effective. Instead of stop smoking, some have stated the medicine is not working. Regardless of how much medicine or breathing treatments you take, smoking with any lung disease can worsen it and increase the risk of other conditions, including cardiovascular disease and type 2 diabetes.

Minding your own healing, understanding some unhealthy habits can be hard to break and may need additional help, counseling cessation, or resources in that area. For many conditions, medication can only do so much. Proper compliance with prescribed meds, along with counseling, a healthy diet, and lifestyle habits can improve the chances a medication will be effective. Medication should be in addition to healthy diet and lifestyle habits, not instead of them.

If you are under doctor's care and taking prescribed medication,

I encourage you to consult with your doctor before starting a new diet or exercise plan. Your doctor knows you, your history, and your individual needs, so they're equipped to guide you toward the steps that are best for you.

EMPOWERMENT CONFERENCES AND SELF-CARE RETREATS

Along with traveling, exploring more healthy food options, and listening to music I found attending women's conferences and fellowships also helped me navigate through my healing process, self-care, and soul-care journey. Soul-care is a form of self-care that prioritizes feeding the mind, spirit, and soul. Women's conferences provided a platform for women to connect with other women of faith spiritually, emotionally, and socially as we grow deeper in our faith. These conferences bring women together by sharing their experiences and pouring into attendees to uplift, strengthen, support, encourage, pray, and inspire. It also motivates them in their spiritual life, their personal healing journey, or vocation. These events give you an opportunity to build relations with people who share your interest. These platforms are usually led by experts, successful, and knowledgeable speakers that talk about learning how to cultivate a positive mind-set that will help individuals to understand the power of thoughts and how to replace negative ones with uplifting ones. These events also empower you to face your fears, equip you with tools, techniques, resources to create healthier habits, reduce stress, and focus on desired outcomes.

I personally gravitated toward women's conferences that solve a problem, not just one that hype you up. The hype is ok sometimes, but I needed my faith strengthened, I needed my soul poured into, and real tools and strategies to help after I leave the conference.

> Now it happened as they went that He entered a certain village; and a certain woman named Martha welcomed Him into her house. And she had a sister called Mary, who also sat at Jesus' feet and heard His word. But Martha was distracted with much serving, and she approached Him and said, "Lord, do You not care that my sister has left me to serve alone? Therefore, tell her to help me." And Jesus answered and said to her, "Martha, Martha, you are worried and troubled about many things. But one thing is needed, and Mary has chosen that good part, which will not be taken away from her," (Luke 10:38-42).

They both loved and wanted to serve Jesus. Martha to me represents the world. She was so busy and distracted with other things that really had little to no spiritual significance. These can be issues and distractions we deal with every day. Mary valued her time with the Lord, she represents the thirsty, hungry soul that rests at Jesus' feet. Jesus expressed to Martha that she was anxious and worried about many things. He said, "There is need of only one thing. Mary has chosen the better part, and it will not be taken from her."

How easily we become Martha (Martha Syndrome). We can get caught up in the necessary tasks and the self-inflicted stress and work we put on ourselves because of our need for perfection, doing for others, people pleasing, for control, or affirmation from others. It was not that Martha needed to feed Jesus, but for her to recognize she needed to be fed by Jesus. It is not only about doing things for God and others but also about spending time with God, to get poured into, to listen, and learn.

Way too often we neglect our soul-care. We make ourselves so busy that we deliberately neglect dealing with important issues in life, allowing them to fester, when we need to be seeking the great Physician to deal with the internal wounds and spiritual needs in our lives.

FORGIVENESS

> And when you stand praying, if you hold anything against anyone, forgive them, so that your Father in heaven may forgive you your sins," (Mark 11:25-26).

Minding my own healing, I learned forgiveness was an important part of my healing journey and self-care/soul-care. Forgiveness is not an easy process, especially when we have been hurt deeply by someone we love. I had to forgive people that wronged me and weren't sorry for the bad things they did to me, but with time and God's help I did. Unforgiveness is a heavy burden to carry and it's a lot of work. It stays with us and wears us down, affecting many areas of our life. Unforgiveness hinders our healing and grows bitterness and resentment. The weight of unforgiveness will continue to grow, hurting ourselves more than anyone else. They say forgiveness is not for the person that hurt or wronged you, it's for you. That statement is true because the negative emotions and attitude associated with unforgiveness is a stronghold, keeps you oppressed by the enemy and affects you, not the person that hurt you. Forgiveness liberates the soul and is a gift from you to yourself. Lewis Smedes said, "It's like setting a prisoner free and realizing the prisoner was you." Forgiveness is an action or a choice to release an offender from our punishment and entrust it all to God to take care of it.

People who can readily forgive others are much more responsible and satisfied inside than those who hold grudges against others. Research and evidence have shown that forgiveness promotes healing and carries many health benefits including lower blood pressure and heart rate, fewer episodes of depression and anxiety symptoms, improved mood, improved function of the immune system, lower risk of substance abuse, a reduction in chronic pain, enhances our relationships, and can bring peace and happiness.

According to the American Psychological Association, forgiveness is the intentional and conscious decision to release feelings of resentment, bitterness, revenge, or negative emotions toward someone who has hurt you, whether or not they deserve your forgiveness or feel sorry for what they did to you. Forgiveness is not about letting someone off the hook, excusing or forgetting that someone wronged you, nor is it a sign of weakness. It doesn't mean you are completely healed of the effects, and it doesn't mean you have to communicate or reconcile with the person either. Forgiveness is being obedient to God, not a feeling and that is what breaks the enemy's power. The enemy has power, but we must remember that he cannot use his power against us unless we give him the right. Romans 12:21 says, *"Do not be overcome by evil, but overcome evil with good."*

> But to you who are listening I say: Love your enemies, do good to those who hate you, bless those who curse you, pray for those who mistreat you," (Luke 6: 27-28).

Not only is it important to forgive others but we also have to forgive ourselves. Self-forgiveness can be harder to forgive ourselves than it is to forgive those who hurt us because it involves acknowledging past mistakes, shortcomings, regrets, failures, shame, and taking responsibility for them. It's natural to want to avoid them; however, avoiding these feelings and emotions can delay healing and lead to self-doubt, anxiety, depression, and other mental and emotional health issues.

Self-forgiveness is not just about facing and accepting what has happened, but also showing compassion to yourself, understanding that you are human, and everyone makes mistakes. Don't dwell on your mistakes. The past is gone, and you cannot change it. Focus on the present and walk toward the future. Self-forgiveness lets you step into the future without the past holding you back. When you forgive yourself, you liberate yourself from the shackles of the past and begin to move forward.

Self-forgiveness can boost self-esteem, help develop a positive attitude along your healing journey, cultivate a sense of hopefulness, and self-love within.

Self-forgiveness is a process that may take some time and practice. I encourage you to seek help or support from loved ones, church family, therapist, or support groups if you find it challenging to forgive yourself. As you forgive yourself be sure to forgive yourself of the things you didn't know. We can't change our yesterday, but we can change our tomorrow.

RECREATIONAL MARIJUANA, ILLICIT DRUGS, ALCOHOL ABUSE, AND THE EFFECTS IT HAS ON OUR HEALING

Minding my own healing and reflecting, God gave me a revelation decades ago for right now. As a young adult around age eighteen-twenty, my past experiences with marijuana were not pleasant. God revealed to me then the powerful, evil, and demonic effects of weed/marijuana would have on this world particularly Black Americans, their families, and communities. Under the influence of marijuana, the few times I tried it, darkness was exposed. I saw demons and people with horns. I was also able to discern people with evil and dark hearts.

I remember a time around age twenty I was at home with my brother and cousin, Moe, when I decided to take a couple puffs of a blunt with them. Shortly after, I needed some household supplies and food items and asked my cousin, Moe, to take me to the store. He took me to the store a couple blocks away from my house. I went into the store, grabbed the few items I needed, and proceeded to walk toward the counter to checkout. Minding my own business walking to the checkout line, I heard a young lady using profanity and cursing somebody out. I didn't bother checking to see who she was yelling at because it wasn't my business, I just wanted to get the items I needed and get back home. While I was paying for my items, the young lady that was yelling and cursing someone out walked up to me, looked me in my eyes and said, "I will see you outside!" I looked behind me to see who she was talking to because I knew she couldn't be talking to me. I didn't know her, say anything, or do anything to her. I never made eye contact with her or anyone in the store until checkout. A young man that was behind me asked, "Do you know her?" My response was, "No, she's not talking to me." I walked out of the store and saw her standing next to a black SUV with a few little kids in her backseat parked next to my cousin's car. As I was getting back into the car she reached into the SUV, pulled out a gun, pointed it through our window toward me, and said, "Now what B***h, what do you have to say now?" She pulled the hammer back on the gun, pointed it at me from the driver's side window, making threats to my cousin that she was going to blow my head off because I disrespected her and she is tired of people disrespecting her. My cousin, Moe, pleaded with her not to shoot, put the gun down, and apologized on my behalf for whatever I did.

Moe convinced her to put the gun down by using reverse psychology telling her how beautiful she was, I wasn't worth it, her kids in the car crying watching her, and what effects this would have on her kids. The girl started crying and began apologizing for what she had done. She said she thought I had said something disrespectful to her in the store about her race and other things. Clearly, she was battling some internal issues if she thought I was being disrespectful and had a conversation with her in the store about her race. I never looked at her or said a word to her in the store. Her mind deceived her to believe I was a threat and her enemy and that I should be killed. Thanks to God and my cousin who saved my life that night. From that day it was confirmation to never smoke weed ever again or try any illicit drugs. And since then, I never did or attempted to.

Since then, I would always talk to my kids about the

importance and dangers of smoking marijuana or other drugs because of the effects it would have on them and the world. I started talking to them about marijuana and what God revealed to me about it when they were very young. I stressed very often to them not to use it, that it is a potential gateway drug that can lead to many unwanted life challenges and health issues.

I know everyone is wired differently, people can use marijuana and not have any issues with it, just like some people can drink alcohol and not get addicted to it nor does it dominate their life. However, this marijuana, weed, cannabis, dope, medical marijuana, or whatever you want to call it, is a beast, it's a whole other entity. I'm pretty sure I'm going to get some backlash on this one, but these are my thoughts, my beliefs, my experience, my research, and revelation while minding my own healing. A lot of people may not want to believe or agree with what I have to say about marijuana and its effects, but these are evidence-based facts I learned and are very important to your healing. If you haven't already, I encourage you to research, educate, and evaluate the effects of marijuana or other drugs as it relates to your mind, body, and healing.

Although doctors prescribe marijuana and it has some medicinal purposes, this content is significant to recreational use of it. In my experience working in the emergency department in the inner city of Detroit for almost fourteen years, I have seen just about everything you can imagine, especially with substance induced health issues and mental illness. It's no secret and evident that there has been a tremendous rise in mental illness. The concern for me is the rise in mental illness in our youth. I've never seen so many kids and young adults battling anxiety, depression, psychosis, bipolar disorder, suicidal and homicidal thoughts. Most of them struggle, finding it hard to navigate life and getting their basic needs met. From what I see on a day-to-day basis on working with these individuals is that at least ninety percent of them, if not all, share something in common. That significant commonality they all share is the use of marijuana. Some may use other illicit drugs or alcohol in addition to marijuana as well. Usually, it's either they only smoke marijuana (including edibles) and don't use other drugs, or they use other drugs including marijuana.

People use marijuana for many reasons like to improve their mood, relax, ease pain (physical and emotional), sleep, increase appetite, and other things, but most people use it for the euphoric high feeling. Just like any other drug, marijuana can be both harmful and addictive. Marijuana often helps people relax and relieve stress and anxiety, so it must be good for people with anxiety, right? Unfortunately, the answer is no. While it is true that the drug can produce an immediate decrease in anxiety, once the immediate effects wear off, people typically experience an increase in anxiety. In fact, regular marijuana use may slowly ramp up anxiety between each use. This is why there has been an overwhelming increase in people that use marijuana develop new anxiety disorders or an increase in anxiety attacks. Marijuana is a depressant and is known to worsen depression.

Marijuana has mind altering compounds that affect both your brain and body, which can be addictive. The addictive component of marijuana is more common than ever these days and one of the biggest struggles for users to overcome. I hear this very often from users, "I could quit if I wanted to, but I just don't want to." Or "I've been smoking weed for years; this has nothing to do with me smoking weed." This attitude tends to ensure a long-term pattern of drug use. The main psychoactive ingredient in marijuana is tetrahydrocannabinol also known as THC that stimulates the part of the brain that responds to pleasure, like food and sex. It unleashes a chemical called dopamine, which gives you that euphoric, relaxed feeling.

The Centers for Disease Control and Prevention states under "Teens" article states the teen brain is still actively developing and continues to develop until around age twenty-five. Marijuana use during adolescence and young adulthood may harm the developing brain. Using marijuana at a young age increases your risk of psychosis, schizophrenia, or other mental conditions. Increase use of marijuana is leading to increased psychosis and bipolar mania. This risk is higher in young men, particularly in African American (Black) males, especially those 16 to 25 years of age. It's no surprise today we see a large growing number of young Black males developing mental illness around this age in our communities. Greater in communities of minorities. You probably know someone if not several people right now battling some kind of mental illness.

One of the most common things I hear when a family member brings their loved ones to the hospital for new onset of bizarre behavior, poor hygiene, hallucinating, paranoia, aggressive, or violent behavior issues is that they usually say, "Something is wrong, they are not acting right, I think somebody drugged them or laced their weed." Not understanding this could be the effects of them just using marijuana. You may have seen some small signs sooner that something is off with them, but often you don't see it developing or know what's happening until it's too late. This is not the case for everyone, sometimes it could be an underlying medical condition that causes change in behavior or mental status, especially in the elderly. I'm referencing the effects and impact marijuana has on the body and brain. It opens doors to demonic attacks. Studies show once you develop schizophrenia, stopping marijuana use may not make the condition or its symptoms go away. Most people that frequently use marijuana can't stop on their own and are in denial of being addicted to it. They usually don't believe it has any relation to their mental or medical illness.

There are increasing numbers of patients and cases treated and being reported of a mysterious condition linked to cannabis and the hallmark symptoms are unexplained or spontaneous vomiting, nausea, severe stomach pain, in severe cases vomiting blood requiring hospitalization and long-term gastrointestinal issues.

An article published by The National Library of Medicine states the recent rise in marijuana legalization and overall increase of marijuana use there have been an increase in patient diagnosis of Cannabinoid Hyperemesis Syndrome (CHS) presented in emergency departments. This usually develops in people who use cannabis frequently over a period of time. In most cases with CHS treatment involves completely stopping cannabis use and symptom management. Unlike with cannabis-induced mental illness, stopping cannabis use will not make the condition go away.

The marijuana being used today is not the same as my generation or before. Studies show it hasn't been for at least two decades. Why? Because the tetrahydrocannabinol (THC), the main psychoactive/mind-altering component of cannabis strains (the part that gets you high) has changed, mutated, and been manipulated over and over.

Keith Humphry, Stanford University Professor of Psychiatry and Drug Policy Advisor to Bush and Obama, testified to a Rhode Island state senate committee that THC concentration has increased over 20% from the eighties to 2017. According to the New York Times, in 2023 those numbers are nearing 100% THC. As the weed gets stronger so do the effects. Studies have shown the harmful effects of marijuana are more prevalent in African Americans particularly African American males.

According to Forbes, marijuana has gone corporate and is now a twenty-billion-dollar industry and growing. There is a lot of money on the line and vested interest to make sure you don't hear the bad things, harmful effects and how it is destroying our people, our communities, our families, our minds, our health, and healing. It doesn't surprise me that there are marijuana dispensaries on just about every corner in most urban neighbor-hoods and Black communities. Though it's not heroin or crack cocaine, its effects can be dangerous and oppressive to our communities and souls. There's nothing "recreational" about it.

Christians are all required to be good stewards of what God has entrusted to us. This includes our earthly bodies. Unfortunately, illicit drug use and alcohol abuse is an extremely effective way to destroy one's health, not just physically, but mentally and emotionally as well. Stay away from anything that will confuse your thoughts, weaken you in any way, make you more vulnerable to sin, and can delay your healing. God is not against pleasure. He wants us to enjoy life and have it to the full. But He knows that the "pleasures of sin" eventually take us further than we want to go and cost us more than we want to pay.

> Be very careful, then, how you live not as un-wise but as wise, making the most of every opportunity, because the days are evil," (Ephesians 5:15-16).

God wants our thought life under His control. The battle for sin always starts in the mind. It's a battle that goes on in our mind between good and evil. Drugs, alcohol abuse, and giving in to our sinful nature cripple our ability to fight off demonic attacks and spiritual warfare. They offer only counterfeit to an abundant and fulfilled life.

If you or a loved one are struggling with addiction, help is available 24/7. The **Substance Abuse and Mental Health Services Administration National Hotline** call **1-800-662-HELP (4357).** You can also call or text **988** someone today. It is never too late to get help, it's never too late to start minding your own healing.

Chapter Seven

SPIRITUAL WARFARE

> For we wrestle not against flesh and blood, but against principalities, against powers, against the rulers of the darkness of this world, against spiritual wickedness in high places."
> (Ephesians 6:12)

Inding my own healing, I learned life is a spiritual war. We face spiritual battles on a daily basis rather major or small against the adversary and enemies of God. These enemies include satan the prince of this world, his minions, demonic forces, and sin. It can be lust of the eyes, lust of the flesh, pride, allurement of sinful pleasures, temptation of drugs, alcohol, sinful thoughts, and sinful behaviors. Spiritual warfare is the battle of over souls. Satan wants nothing more than to bring defeat, for his main purpose is to steal, kill, and destroy.

> The thief cometh not, but for to steal, and to kill, and to destroy I am come that they might have life, and that they might have it more abundantly," (John 10:10).

I learned spiritual battles are not fought by worldly weapons, not by might, nor by the power of man, but with the power of God and His spirit.

> For though we live in the world, we do not wage war as the world does. The weapons we fight with are not the weapons of the world. On the contrary, they have divine power to demolish stronghold. We demolish arguments and every pretension that sets itself up against the knowledge of God, and we take captive every thought to make it obedient to Christ," (2 Corinthians 10:3-5).

FULL ARMOR OF GOD

God provides the powerful armor of God to protect us. Each piece of the armor of God is essential, and the Bible tells us how to put them on and use them effectively.

> Put on the full armor of God, so that you can take your stand against the devil's schemes. For our struggle is not against flesh and blood, but against the rulers, against the authorities, against the

powers of this dark world and against the spiritual forces of evil in the heavenly realms. Therefore, put on the full armor of God, so that when the day of evil comes, you may be able to stand your ground, and after you have done everything, to stand. Stand firm then, with the belt of truth buckled around your waist, with the breastplate of righteousness in place, and with your feet fitted with the readiness that comes from the gospel of peace. In addition to all this, take up the shield of faith, with which you can extinguish all the flaming arrows of the evil one. Take the helmet of salvation and the sword of the Spirit, which is the word of God. And pray in the Spirit on all occasions with all kinds of prayers and requests. With this in mind, be alert and always keep on praying for all the Lord's people," (Ephesians 6:11-18).

MINDING YOUR OWN
HEALING JOURNEY

> *Do not conform to the pattern of this world, but be transformed by the renewing of your mind. Then you will be able to test and approve what God's will is, his good, pleasing and perfect will,"* (Romans 12:2).

Minding my own healing, I learned it is important to set my thoughts on the things of God and not of this world, to not have a world-focus mind-set to define my character, values, and not desiring to live like everyone else. Instead focus on my healing, wholeness and renewing my mind, being transformed from the inside out by changing how I think so I can begin to understand God's will for my life. Focus on my healing and being the light of this world no matter what is going on. Plan to outdo my past, not other people, live life from a healed space, and live life on purpose.

 He heals the brokenhearted and binds up their wounds," (Psalm 147:3)

God is reminding us that His power is unlimited. He is mighty enough to heal all wounds no matter when or how they occurred in our lives. Our pain is not beyond His tremendous power. He is the Great Physician, able to reach into our past and heal our souls. The scripture says, *"He heals,"* meaning this healing is ongoing. It is not a one-time deal but rather a supernatural act that can occur over and over in the lives of the brokenhearted, for as much and as long as we need healing.

Set your thoughts on the things of God. Begin every day by setting your mind on the wonderful character of the living God, immerse yourself in the word of God and meditate on it. Does that mean we will never have bad days? No! But we will not live expecting them. God doesn't promise us life will be easy. In fact, he warns us there will be difficult times here on earth. Some people get disappointed and discouraged when they get saved and find themselves still struggling with healing, overcoming challenges, and temptation to sin. There is a myth or presumption that some people think when they become saved or turned their life over to the Lord, that immediately things are supposed to be perfect. That life will be easy, they won't struggle, and won't be tempted by sin; and that's not true. Yet, we serve a God who was tempted, with all respect was perfect, without blemish, and did not sin. God did promise coming to him we will have power to flee from sin, heal, and we will have hope and encouragement from the scriptures, from the prophets, the Psalms, the Holy Spirit, and from the church to help us overcome all power of the enemy.

There is no brokenness that's too shattered for God's healing touch. He knows how we feel. He felt the hurt and the pain. He knows it was unfair and maybe cruel. He knows the weight you are carrying. God loves you and he promise to walk with you through it all.

Bring God your brokenness, your trauma, your mourning, your spiritual heaviness, bring him your ashes. He will replace your ashes of life with the beauty of His presence.

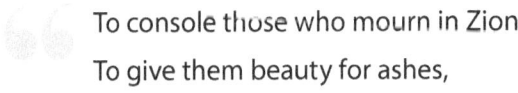

> To console those who mourn in Zion,
> To give them beauty for ashes,
> The oil of joy for mourning,
> The garment of praise for the spirit of heaviness;
> That they may be called trees of righteousness,

The planting of the LORD, that He may be glori-
fied." (Isaiah 63:1)

It's never too late to do better, it's never too late to be better, it's never too late to start minding your own healing. We can't change our yesterday, but we can change our tomorrow. It's either one day or day one— you choose.

The pain, trauma, or brokenness may not have been your fault, but the healing is your responsibility. Remember, unhealed and hurt people hurt others, but healed people can heal others.

I pray the personal stories and testimonies in the next pages shared from the beautiful hearts and souls of others and their experiences with past trauma and minding their own healing will inspire, encourage, and motivate you to begin or continue minding your own healing.

TAMIKA CHEREE HENRY

Tamika Cheree Henry, a writer, speaker, and mental health and domestic violence awareness advocate, was born and raised in Detroit, MI. Tamika is the founder of I Am Here, a 501(c)(3) nonprofit organization who is committed to helping survivors of violent tragedies and domestic violence heal and rebuild their lives. Tragedy was an early part of Tamika's life. After experiencing the death of her mother, father, and her only child she knew that she was called to do work and help others. I Am Here was birthed out of the most painful loss that any parent could experience the loss of her only child. Three years of great faith and courage, coupled with walking through her own grief and healing, resulted in the manifestation of this organization. Tamika's walk and journey led her to this new passion, helping people turn tragedy into triumph. Tamika holds a Bachelor of Science degree in Communication from Purdue University

Global. Tamika currently resides in Missouri with her husband of ten years.

STAY CONNECTED WITH TAMIKA

I Am Here, "Helping survivors heal and rebuild, mind, body, and soul, after violent tragedies."
Tamika Cheree Henry, Founder

Phone: 314-877-8371
Email: iamhereorg15@gmail.com
Web: iamhere15.org

I Am Here Nonprofit Organization
P.O Box 1085 Florissant, MO 63032

MINDING MY OWN HEALING POST TRAUMA LIFE AFTER DEATH

BY TAMIKA CHEREE HENRY

The experience of grief is such a deep, layered, and emotional journey that doesn't come with a specific end date and is often challenging to articulate but I'm going to give it my best shot. I have often said I don't own the patent on pain and grief; however, I have experienced my fair share of both. I wish I could say that 2015 was my first introduction of the loss of one I loved so dearly, but it wasn't. I experienced my first major loss when I was 4 years old and then again at 5 and so many more followed from that point on. It wasn't until January 11, 2015, 57 days after my wedding, 17 days after Christmas, 10 days after the New Year, and 6 days after my 40th birthday that I experienced the greatest loss; the most prevalent heartbreak, the deepest pain— a death that alters the rest of your life. I lost my only child, Jazmyne Lyniece Gibson, at the hands of one who claimed to love her. As my 21-year-old daughter was in the prime of her life as a student and entrepreneur, her then boyfriend picked up a gun and shot her in the kitchen as she cooked. When I was 4, my mother was shot in the head and killed in our home. Less than a year later, 7 months after the death of my mother my father was shot and killed as he came home from work. I lost both sets of my grandparents, lost 13 aunts and uncles and many others before Jazzy's death. Despite my early experience with the amount of death I had previously faced, there was absolutely nothing that could prepare me for this.

Jazzy's death shook my very existence and purpose. I've avoided putting this on paper because it's truly painful and each new step I take also confirms the loss I've suffered. However, I refuse to allow what I've walked through to be in vain. I refuse to let suffering be just suffering, to let death simply be death— to let loss be the end. I am crazy enough to believe that nothing I've been through was wasted.

HOW DID I GET HERE?

My daughter, Jazmyne Lyniece Gibson, affectionately known as Jazz, Jazzy, or Gibby was born on March 5, 1993. I was 17 when I got pregnant and I gave birth two months after my 18th birthday. She was a 21-year-old college student, an entrepreneur, and in the prime of her life. After the unfortunate tragedy at Sandyhook Elementary School, Jazz knew exactly what she wanted to major in, Child Psychology. After looking at the faces of those young innocent children, she wanted to help children just like them. She loved children. In December of 2014, our first Christmas together as a blended family, we planned out the next few years of our lives as mother and daughter. We made promises to one another and set goals regarding school and business. I told her that I was going back to college, and we would be college graduates together. Jazzy's dream was cut short at the hands of someone who decided to pick up a gun, aim it, and pull the trigger. I knew that it was my responsibility to finish what she was unable to and there was no doubt that I would walk across the stage with a degree in my hand.

In February of 2015, one month after her death, I started my classes. I had never been so committed to finishing school as I was during this part of my educational journey. It was extremely challenging as I dealt with the overwhelming amount of grief, being present for others that were hurting, in addition to dealing with the legal matters concerning her death. I dealt with PTSD, depression, and medical concerns while keeping up with deadlines, posts, and writing papers. In August of 2015, I lost 3 people within a two-week period— a dear cousin, Darlene, one of my closest friends and prayer partners, Desiree "Desi" and my god-dad, the legendary Mel Farr Sr. During Papa Farr's visitation, I sat in the parking lot of the funeral home and attended class. Throughout the next 6 ½ years the road was filled with breaks for my mental health, grades I wasn't proud of, late nights reminding myself of the pep talks I would give Jazz when times got rough for her. I prayed for continued strength and endurance. In November of 202,1 I submitted my last paper and in May of 2022 I walked across the stage for both of us. I knew I didn't walk alone, and I didn't just walk for me. I walked for my greatest love, Jazmyne Lyniece Gibson. I walked for those watching, praying they would be inspired.

From January of 2015 through October 2015 as I balanced being a wife, school, and several unfavorable medical diagnoses, I traveled from California to Michigan to deal with court dates and ultimately the sentencing of the person who took Jazzy's life. On Saturday, January 17, 2015, I buried my most cherished gift and on Monday, October 5, 2015, I sat in a courtroom as the one who had taken her life learned his fate— 15 to 50 years in prison. Some would call this closure, but did closure ever really exist when someone took the life of your greatest love? A life that was not theirs to take. Two lives destroyed and two families shattered by tragedy— there was no rejoicing in the courtroom. Instead of cheers there were tears. Hugs replaced high fives. Hugs between two families that were broken. Hugs between two mothers that were crushed by the weight of catastrophe. I don't call it closure; I call it the aftermath.

IT'S PERSONAL

As I approached March 5, 2015, Jazzy's first birthday after her death, I didn't know what to expect. I proceeded with caution and with much prayer. I wasn't fearful, but I braced myself for any emotions that I may have felt. I told myself that whatever I felt that day would be ok. I told myself that I was entitled to any emotion that I would face, and that I would be ok. I gave myself my own pep talk. I told myself to cry if I needed to, to laugh if I wanted, to sing regardless of who heard me, to dance even if others were watching, to pray like I've always done and to take time to celebrate My Angel in whatever fashion I chose. I gave myself grace because I understood that this life that I now live is completely new to me and would never be the same.

I learned early on to give myself grace, to allow myself the space to grieve and live, to laugh and cry, to be happy and sad. God spoke to my heart early in the process encouraging me to embrace every emotion. Grief is an essential part of the healing process. I began to understand that everything I felt, every emotion was necessary and that I owned them. Sadness was mine, but so was joy. Tears were mine, but so was laughter. Anger belonged to me, but so did forgiveness. I had to spend time with my sadness, sit down with it at times, and then I released it, knowing that it would come back again when it was time. The longer we prolong the time needed with these emotions the longer it takes to heal.

QUICK FIXES DON'T EXIST

It is a humanistic response for people to look for an immediate remedy to the pain they are experiencing. When we are in physical pain, we generally do two things: we try to alleviate the pain or we try to identify the source of the pain so that we can take measures to prevent the pain from moving forward. So, it is quite natural when we experience loss, and that loss is coupled with not only emotional pain but can also bring about physical pain, we search for the quickest way to alleviate the pain. People have often asked me how I do it or what did I do, but what I found most often is that they are looking for the "thing" that will eliminate the pain in that moment. Honestly, I wish I could offer those suffering a quick fix, but the truth is they don't exist. I've learned that grief is a journey not a destination, moving from one place in the process to another. The harsh reality is no matter what you do, the sting of this type of loss will linger. It has a lasting effect that I will feel for the rest of the life I live.

In the beginning, each moment felt like an insurmountable unachievable task. It hurt to breath. To get through each minute, hour and day was nothing short of a miracle. When I made it through another week, I felt as if I had achieved the impossible. As I pushed my way, determined to LIVE, I saw weeks turn into months and months became years and I knew I didn't walk alone. I learned to be patient with myself, understanding that no two years would be the same.

Easter of 2024, nine years and three months after my Jazzy was taken from us I experienced something completely different than I did the year before. I was extremely sad, married, and yet still very sad. As I cooked, I was sad. I struggled through physical and emotional pain. I didn't want to talk to anyone. I tried putting my phone on "Do Not Disturb" (DND) because even those who I hold the closest to, I did not want to talk to them. I was reminded as families were coming together to share in the love and joy with one another that I didn't have my daughter to share in the joy of the day. I had a keen sense of awareness this day and what I did, how I managed, and what I felt, it was as if God had heightened my senses. As I cooked, I listened to my church back home and continued the rest of my time cooking listening to gospel music and cried and cooked and cried and cooked. I felt her loss on this day in a way that I hadn't felt in a long time.

During the last 9 years of navigating my new normal and my healing exploration, there were countless lessons I learned. I learned that God truly is my strength. I don't mean this to sound like a cliché, but He truly is, and He has been strength for me in my weakest hours. God also gave me therapy as a resource to be utilized for as long as I need it. I needed God and therapy to process my loss and heartache. I also learned my village mattered. Those with whom you surround yourself make an incredible difference. Lastly, after reflecting on countless losses I recognized that I had a choice, I could choose to drown in my grief or turn pain into purpose. I chose to pull purpose out of my pain because pain also served a purpose.

BUT GOD?

I can honestly say I remember my first encounter with God at the age of 5. Halfway through the age of 5 I had lost both my mother and my father, and I can recall a loving presence with me even in my saddest hours. I would rock and I would cry, but I would also pray. Even though God did not take the pain from me, I knew He was there with me, His presence surrounded me. Although I knew God, felt His presence, had a relationship with God for as long as I could naturally recall, the death of my daughter, Jazmyne, shook my very foundation and everything I knew about life and God came into question. Despite my inability to think straight, I was able to call on the name of Jesus. Sometimes calling His name was literally the only prayer I could pray. On the days where the thought of my loss took my breath away I "somehow" managed to cry out in agony to God my Father. It was during that time that my brokenness ushered into a deeper level of praise that gave me supernatural strength. This was not easy by any means. The depth of the pain went deep, but God's presence was there amid the gut-wrenching cry. It was there where He was healing me.

GOD AND THERAPY

It has often been stated that "The Year of Firsts" is the most difficult year after losing your loved one; however, what I found was that any year after the loss can been extremely challenging to navigate because it is truly the rest of your life that you are forced to reconcile with the reality that for every birthday, holiday, major accomplishment, birth, and yes even death they are not there to share in the joy and grief with you. For me, everything was defined before Jazz was taken and after Jazz died.

Days after burying Jazz, I told my family that I was going to need therapy. I knew that in conjunction with my faith in God I was going to need the expertise of a therapist. I realized early on I had to be a willing participant in my own healing. Just as there are stages in grief there were also stages in my therapeutic journey.

After crying in my sessions for about 6 weeks straight, I recognized I wanted more, I needed more. As agonizing as I was to imagine a life without Jazz, I knew I had to find a way to live after her death. I took time to read the word of God and begin journaling. I sought out a therapist that could give me more, provide me with techniques to deal with my trauma. I made therapy an essential part of my life. I wanted to help with managing my PTSD, I needed to know I would not always be paralyzed by my grief.

There are so many misconceptions that people have when someone suffers a great loss such as this. I've often heard phrases like, "well at least you have your husband," or "at least you're not alone," and it's even been said that, "I got over losing Jazz quickly." The response to some of these phrases is a book for another day. I learned quickly that it was imperative to surround myself with those who were authentic about their desire for you to heal in a healthy way. I had to take measures to protect my environment and make peace a priority by limiting who I engaged in conversation with and by preserving some relationships and understanding the season for some relationships had ended.

PURPOSE OUT OF PAIN

The reality is that I will live with the loss of my Jazz for the rest of my life, and I had some difficult choices to make. The first choice was the choice of love and forgiveness as a part of my healing journey. I know there are many who will never understand my love and compassion for the family whose son took the life of Jazzy, but that's ok, it's my cross to bear and my story to share. Forgiveness does not take away the hurt. It will not take away the pain. It will not bring my Jazzy back, but it frees me! It frees my heart to love! It frees my soul!

I was determined to transform my grief into something that was bigger than me. I vowed not to allow Jazzy's life nor her death to be in vain. I will honor her memory so that I will not be paralyzed by her death.

On March 5, 2015, Jazzy's 22nd birthday, I met with a mentor— a friend who was more like a sister and I shared with her what was in my heart. I knew that God had not walked with me through the violent tragedies of both my mother and my father, surviving sexual, domestic, and intimate partner violence and now the death of my beloved daughter without purpose in mind. I knew I had to speak out. I've always been an advocate for mental health and therefore I knew I had to advocate for those who had survived violent tragedies and domestic violence. I've often heard that "Your greatest loss or pain is often the launching pad for calling, your purpose," so out of my most painful heartbreak "I Am Here" was born.

I Am Here is a nonprofit organization that helps survivors of domestic violence and violent tragedies heal and rebuild their lives. Realizing the gap that existed between individuals leaving abusive situations and/or surviving the death of loved ones, and those individuals healing and learning to live again. I Am Here has provided assistance to cover or offset the cost of therapeutic services, provided food and clothing vouchers as well as helped provide basic in-home needs.

My purpose and my mission is that someone will see me and know that there is life after death. I make it a point to see God in EVERYTHING. I am intentional about taking walks and appreciating the beauty around me. I attend a yearly girls trip every October with my family and friends and give myself permission to laugh and be in the moment as much as I possibly can. I started a nonprofit organization to remember and honor Jazz while helping others heal. I fill the most fulfillment when I am giving back to others. I take time to pour into those coming behind me dealing with domestic violence and mothers grieving from the loss of a child or children. I'm not an expert on life, survival, or domestic violence but what I am is a by-product of God's love, and God's faithfulness. I Am Here, a survivor turning tragedy into triumph.

ALAJIA TURNER

*A*lajia Turner was born and raised in Inkster, Michigan. She graduated from Wayne County Community College District with an Associate Degree in General Studies and certified in Addiction Studies. Alajia is currently pursuing a Bachelor's Degree in Psychology at Wayne State University. She is an active member of People's Community Baptist church in Westland, Michigan where she serves as an assistant teacher in the junior church. She is also a faith-based motivational speaker.

STAY CONNECTED WITH ALAJIA

Email: Alajia42@gmail.com
Phone: 248-606-8926
Instagram: @alajiaaaa_____
Facebook: Alajia Turner
Tiktok: @alajiaaa_____
Website: https://linktr.ee/sayitoncemorepodcast?utm_source=link tree_profile_share&ltsid=7b49e83e-32d7-4774-a76e-79589be6cb66

MINDING MY OWN HEALING

BY ALAJIA TURNER

It was February 16, 2019, when my life changed. In fact, I thought my life was over. Me and four friends were leaving a party at 3 a.m., intoxicated and under the influence. Heading home, the driver began to drive erratically, and he instantly started to speed. It was all fun and games until it wasn't. As we began to yell at him to slow the car down, he just wouldn't budge. I began to call upon the name of the Lord to save and help me out of this situation. Before I got in the car with them, I had a funny feeling that I shouldn't go with them, but I ignored it. Going nearly 100 mph he cut off another car on the service drive, lost control of the wheel, and we crashed into a building. I had loss consciousness, not knowing how long I had been out, I woke up to the paramedics saying, "We are going to get you guys out, but we have to cut the car door open." It was at that moment I knew that my life was done. While being rushed to the hospital they cut my pants off, had to give me oxygen, and connected me to a heart monitor for vital signs. The pain, fear, and hopelessness I felt was indescribable. I couldn't stop crying and screaming.

Arriving at the hospital, I was transferred to another bed and instantly felt deep pain throughout my entire body. The doctors tried to calm me down and reassure me that I made it safely, but I was confused and not in my right state of mind. They began running tests, I later found out I had sustained multiple fractures in my neck, back, and to my right femur bone. I had lost so much blood they had to give me an emergency blood transfusion.

Being in the hospital and doing rehab, I had to relearn how to walk again. You would think during that time that I would have repent and rededicated my life to God and turned away from my wicked and worldly ways, but that wasn't how the story unfolded. I had to hit below rock bottom for my eyes to fully open. Four months after being home from the hospital everything started to kick in and process rapidly. I had gone back to self-medicating, using marijuana while being severely depressed, suicidal, and paranoid thinking people were out to get me. I fell out with my friends, went through an unhealthy and toxic breakup while dealing with a consecutive series of trials and tribulations. I got sick and tired of all the pain and tears. I needed a change and knew my life needed to be turned around. I grew bitter. I went into a closet and screamed and cried at God, and at myself for all what was happening to me.

It was when I cried out to God to change me and to take away this pain and guilt I was feeling and had never felt before. It was then I knew I needed to rededicate my life to God and repent. I had to realize that people could only encourage me, but they couldn't change me. I'm grateful that I reconnected with someone who could. God was my only hope. I had no one else to lean on. God pulled me up out of that dump and started cleaning me up. This was when my true healing process began.

Minding my own healing, I learned to trust God and believed He would do just what He said he would do. I attended physical and mental health therapy. I began building myself up with prayer and faith-based motivational sermons and I rejoined my child-hood church home. I didn't think that I would ever heal properly nor did I think I would stop smoking, partying, and living life my way. But God had other plans for me. I would have never been able to let go of my old life and receive healing without the love, grace and mercy of God, my family prayers, and the support from a team of therapists. My obedience to God was necessary before I could start taking the steps to claim and begin my healing journey. I had my doubts, but I was determined.

Minding my own healing, I look back over my life and I see God had his hand on me all along, He did just what he promised. He healed me, He changed me, He delivered, and set me free from the bondage of sin. The journey to healing won't always be easy but when you trust and partner with the healer, He makes it worth it.

> But he said to me, "My grace is sufficient for you, for my power is made perfect in weak-ness. Therefore I will boast all the more gladly about my weaknesses, so that Christ's power may rest on me," (2 Corinthian 12:9).

TERESA CREGGETT-MOORE

Teresa Creggett-Moore known to many as "TT" was born in Detroit, Michigan and raised by a single mother. She is the oldest of four children. She is the wife to Swifty McVay from D12 one of Eminem's platinum rap groups from Detroit and the mother of two awesome sons, Markell and Kody.

Teresa has a podcast show called "TTfromTheD" on Spotify, IHeart Radio, Amazon Music, and wear many hats. You can find out more about her creative gifts by visiting her website: www.ttfromthed.com.

Teresa has been active in the entertainment world for over thirty years. She is an accomplished versatile and experienced actress, producer, stage manager, director, artist assistant, MC, event coordinator, podcaster, and manager assistant.

One of her favorite sayings is, "I get the job done." If you have had the opportunity to work with her, you will find her saying to be tried and true.

MINDING MY OWN HEALING

BY TERESA CREGGETT-MOORE

Minding my own healing, I learned one must take full responsibility and choose to want to heal. I have asked myself, "Are you ready to deal with some sad times, scary memories, open to dealing with any hidden unresolved inner hurt, anger, or hatred?" I would have to say yes. I have come to understand in my years here on earth that our life is not our own and it is meant to be lived outside your body and inside your heart.

You may know me as this outgoing, funny, witty, and gifted woman who can walk into any room and join any conversation, but let me remind you that I was not always laughing and enjoying life with happiness in my heart. Would you believe there were several times I attempted to end my own life from the heaviness of what was going on behind the four walls of my house.

It is funny how tragic situations can happen in a house and neighbors, family, and friends would say, they don't believe it from the lack of seeing the ugly truth. There was a Lifetime movie called *If These Walls Could Talk* and I thought to myself, *if these walls of my house could talk, what horrifying stories would they reveal.*

Sit back and take a stroll down memory lane with me for a bit, grab your water, coffee, tea, warm milk, beer, or wine and let me introduce you to the little big girl named Teresa. I am one of four children born to a strong Black woman who just so happens to be a **Domestic Violence Survivor.** What you are about to read will allow you to see how your past does not always dictate your future.

Along my life journey after becoming transparent and using my pain to help heal others, I am what some call a **Domestic Violence Child Survivor.** I do not have any outer scars from the battles witnessed by my little girl eyes; I have spiritual and emotional battle wounds. I learned along my life journey internal scars bleed from time to time, they remind us that healing is a process. I think many people believe healing happens overnight, within a month, or within a year. Truth be told, we heal one internal wound at a time.

There is a cliché saying, "We all have a story". Do you know you're a co-editor of your own story? It is important to recognize when a ghost writer has started writing your story. It is also important to understand we can make edits to our story. I believe you will touch and agree that everyone does not get to make edits. Do you know some victims have been silenced by their abusers then there are those survivors who have chosen to take their trauma to the grave.

Traveling through life we will learn the true understanding of the poetic question many powerful poets ask, "Do you know who shoulders you stand on?" I owe that reminder question to the great Twinkie Clark. I stand on the shoulders of ALL the women around the world who have decided to turn their tragedies into victories.

I remember being a happy little girl who laughed out loud, played with barbie dolls, dressed up in my mother's high heel shoes, and I also remember when my innocence was taken without warning like a thief in the night by a relative. It did not happen abruptly; it was a lot of grooming and thankfully life gave me a quiet blessing and her name is Victoria.

I did not witness domestic violence until I turned eleven years old. I have a rhetorical question for you, what does a child know about trauma, molestation, domestic violence? I think we all can sit back and unpack the answer differently. Statistics show that, 1 in every 4 women will have personally experienced domestic violence or know someone who has experienced domestic violence before they become adults.

I have had to witness my mother being hit in the head with a trophy, metal pipe, and a big bag of dimes. I have witnessed my mother going toe to toe with men who claimed they loved her, cared for her, and would never hurt her. One of the most horrific memories from my trauma-filled childhood was watching helplessly as my mother was body slammed at eight months pregnant on her back.

Do you know what that did to me as a child? It left me feeling angry, filled with hatred watching her being taken away in an ambulance, or healing up quietly behind closed doors. A house divided started to become our norm and I realized life was truly taking me down a dark pathway with no light in sight.

New Years Eve of 1989 changed my life and led me mentally down a pathway that could have had me growing up in the correctional system and/or dead. My mother and younger sibling's dad often had heated arguments; they became so common that it no longer bothered me. One night, they were fighting and tussling. I ran and woke his younger brother up and told him that they were fighting. He ran into the kitchen and separated them. I grabbed my mom and when she stood up her forehead had been split by the pipe laying on the kitchen floor. Things seemed unreal as we ran up the back stairs to the upper part of the house.

I remember grabbing a jagged edge butcher knife with a hook on the tip. I could hear him coming up the back stairs yelling, "Open the f*****g door before I kick it in!" My mother was frantically looking for her keys. I could hear him kicking in the back door and yelling, "No Mom we have to go," and we ran toward the front of the house down the front stairs. We ran to my mother's car; I saw him run out looking our way and he jumped into his car. I kept trying to open the passenger's door of my mother's car, but I forgot it was jammed. We had to climb in and out the window like on the Dukes of Hazzard. I witnessed my mom's car being rammed from behind and knocked into a busy intersection.

I stood in the middle of the street in the freezing snow with only my socks, tank top, and red Levi jeans on— adrenaline was running high. I saw the reverse lights of his car and got scared, ran back toward the house, and dropped my butcher knife— which slid into the sewer. He came running up the stairs, I was filled with hatred and anger. I started cursing at him and he told me to shut my damn mouth, or else he would throw me off the balcony. My siblings were crying, and his brother said, "Please do not say anything else because he is high," and didn't know what else he was capable of doing.

He taunted me and told me to go call my uncle who was a cop and black belt. I ran over to the phone and picked it up, there was no dial tone. I looked at the cord and realized he had pulled it out from the wall. He laughed and said, "You can't call him," and that's when I saw red and blue lights through the window and within minutes the police were coming up the stairs. Two officers entered the house, one asked my stepdad if he was Mr. Cooper and did he assault Mrs. Cooper. He replied, "Yes." They told him to put down my younger siblings. He stood up, they handcuffed him, and placed him under arrest. My mother walked in with another officer with her forehead bleeding. They gave her a big pad to put on her forehead to stop the bleeding. She had a busted lip and her voice was trembling. The police asked him why he assaulted my mom. He told them he planned to kill our whole family and I remember thinking to myself, *wow he was going to kill us.* One night could have been the end of five people's lives at the hand of one man.

The smell of popcorn was a trigger for me. It was a reminder of the night my entire immediate family could have been murdered by the hands of someone who people did not see as a real-life monster. We lived with someone who was a master of manipulation and had narcissist traits. I remember watching the movie *The Burning Bed* with Farrah Faucet over and over and deciding that my mother was blinded by what she thought was love. A few of my mother's girlfriends were also in domestic violent filled relationships. She would give them advice, but she would never tell them about her blood-filled fights. I came from the era where you understood the saying, "A child should be seen and not heard." We certainly looked, listened, but knew to stay in a child's place. I didn't know then that I was an empath, I was that loving person who tried to make people happy, feel safe, yet I looked for love from extended family.

My mother finally made her exit plan, carefully and precisely. We were not allowed to talk about the plan. I understood the plan and although it made me sad, I knew we would have the chance to live life peacefully and without violence. We moved over twenty-five times throughout my childhood, it was not until we relocated to Oak Park in 1990. There, I made friends and did not fear getting evicted or having our lights and water cut off.

My life came to a screeching halt in July of 1994 when my best friend, Annie, was murdered. Annie Johnson was my ride or die sister-friend and we loved each other like sisters. She was also the sister of my first love. I will never forget being woken up out of my sleep and being told that Annie was gone. I didn't get a chance to see or touch her, and not being able to was so heartbreaking.

Annie and I snuck off and did what teenagers did. I recall one night we were down at Belle Isle, and Annie asked me, "What would you do if I died?" I looked at her and said, "I am older so, I am going to die before you." Annie said, "I am serious, you don't know that." I replied, "I would probably come to the cemetery every week and kick it with you, and make sure your tombstone is clean." Several of my childhood friends made poor decisions— some went to prison and some died. I could not take the grief of losing Annie and wanted to leave this life, so I attempted to take my own life the same year. It did not work. I went on grieving quietly and started isolating myself from family and friends. I visited her gravesite every weekend, holiday, and on her birthday. I did exactly what I told her I would do. It was my true broken season in life. I was feeling responsible and guilty for being alive and her being gone.

As the years passed by, I decided I wanted to become a Homicide Detective. I applied at Detroit Police Department and passed my agility test and MCOLES. I did not pass the psychological test after being questioned about my ability to not be a vigilante. They asked, "What would happen if I was dispatched to the area where the gang members who took her life lived?" I said what I thought they needed to hear, and I believe they saw right through me.

I often found myself angry and getting into arguments with peers, I threatened one of them. I was reported to my boss and sent to anger management. I believe it was the overdue season of accountability for me. I had never been to counseling. I always heard people saying, "Only white people go to counseling, Black people don't go to counseling." I found counseling to be beneficial and therapeutic. I learned techniques on how to handle anger, create boundaries, and the power of self-forgiveness.

During my ten years of grieving for Annie, my relationship with God was strained. I found myself feeling alone. I was tired mentally, emotionally, spiritually, and wanting to take a hard pause in life. I was invited to try church again and started to rebuild my relationship with God. I learned that I feared recurrence of domestic violence and realized depression tried to creep back into my life.

Minding my own healing, I realized through counseling and openly speaking about my trials and tribulations that I was a victim of childhood trauma. I held onto anger, depression, and anxiety. I also learned the stages of healing had to manifest. In order to heal properly you must be open to being accountable, transparent, and honest with yourself.

I learned there are five stages of healing from trauma. The **Denial stage** is where I acted like nothing happened. I was able to act like domestic violence was not happening at home but, I could not deny Annie was gone. I do not recall going through the **Bargaining stage**. I was upfront about my **Anger stage**, and wanted the world to know how mad and upset I was. I was able to mask the sadness of witnessing domestic violence but I could not hide the sadness of losing Annie. The **Healing stage,** well, this stage is an ongoing stage. Healing is not meant to be rushed and we must remember to move at our own pace. The last stage is the **Acceptance stage,** and I had no problem accepting what was happening and breaking down my spirit.

I found myself creating my inner protector TT, she has helped guide the woman Teresa along her journey to healing and forgiveness. I sometimes look at childhood photos and think to myself, *the little girl Teresa seems to be gone without a trace.* I am happy to share that she is alive and sits in awe of the woman who survived a very turbulent childhood.

I arrived at a point of understanding some may never understand what it means to have seen more than the eyes could ever see, experience more than the human body was built to endure in their entire lifetime. I have seen and done some things that would have made some lose grip on life and take their own life. I believe in being transparent, there is healing awaiting to be released when we are obedient, decide to walk in our truth, write our own stories, and mind our own healing.

Thank you for reading *Minding My Own Healing*

If you enjoyed this book or found it helpful, please help spread the word by leaving an online review.

KEEP IN TOUCH WITH MELANIE SMILES

WEBSITE: www.MelanieSmiles.com
PHONE: 248-688-6021
EMAIL: info@melaniesmiles.com

Facebook: Melanie Smiles
Instagram: @mel_rnsmiles